Praise for
Create Uniqueness

'In this book Riccardo Pozzoli has managed to dilute in a very simple and practical way all the principles of how to begin a company in these modern times. I recommend it to anyone who aspires to be a first-time entrepreneur. This is the perfect start to building a startup!' SIMON BECKERMAN, FOUNDER, DEPOP

'Packed with witty anecdotes and practical wisdom, *Create Uniqueness* is filled with actionable recommendations that aspiring entrepreneurs will find greatly instructive. Riccardo Pozzoli recounts his entrepreneurial journey from Bocconi student to becoming one of Italy's most admired entrepreneurs and shares all the lessons he learned along the way.' SANDRINE CRENER-RICARD, CO-AUTHOR, THE BLONDE SALAD CASE STUDY

'Riccardo Pozzoli is a creative thinker who inspires those who meet and learn from him to find new ways of engaging with the world. His genuine belief and passion for turning new ideas into successful businesses is rooted in his commitment to being modern in his outlook on life: he can predict trends and monetize ideas but realizes that the path to success is inextricably linked to understanding that resonating with others on a human and compassionate level is more important than anything.' NANA SARIAN, GENERAL COUNSEL, FASHION INDUSTRY

Create Uniqueness

How to turn a passion into a business

Riccardo Pozzoli

KoganPage

First published in Italy in 2018 as *Non è un lavoro per vecchi* by DeA Planeta Libri S.r.l
Published in Great Britain and the United States in 2019 as *Create Uniqueness* by Kogan Page Limited

2nd Floor, 45 Gee Street	122 W 27th St, 10th Floor	4737/23 Ansari Road
London	New York, NY 10001	Daryaganj
EC1V 3RS	USA	New Delhi 110002
United Kingdom		India

www.koganpage.com

World copyright © 2019 DeA Planeta Libri S.r.l, Novara

The right of Riccardo Pozzoli and of each commissioned author of this work to be identified as an author of this work has been asserted by them in accordance with the Copyright, Designs and Patents Act 1988.

Translated from Italian to English by Vanessa Di Stefano.

ISBNs
Hardback	978 1 78966 018 0
Paperback	978 0 7494 9738 5
Ebook	978 0 7494 9737 8

British Library Cataloguing-in-Publication Data

A CIP record for this book is available from the British Library.

Library of Congress Cataloging-in-Publication Data

CIP data is available. Library of Congress Control Number: 2019028008

Typeset by Integra Software Services, Pondicherry
Print production managed by Jellyfish
Printed and bound by CPI Group (UK) Ltd, Croydon CR0 4YY

Contents

CONTENTS

CONTENTS

About the author

Riccardo Pozzoli is a young Italian entrepreneur. He graduated in finance from the Bocconi University in Milan, and at the age of 23 he founded, together with Chiara Ferragni, *The Blonde Salad*, one of the most popular and influential fashion blogs ever worldwide. Since then, he has given birth to other startups in the fields of fashion, communication and food, and he has no intention of stopping. Riccardo today is also advising global enterprises about marketing and innovation, giving lectures at international business schools, and mentoring young entrepreneurs!

Preface

Being old is not an age thing:

Those who are old are those who do not want to get involved, who do not take a chance on themselves, who are afraid to change their minds.

One of the most celebrated Italian startuppers tells the story of the new generation of entrepreneurs, the end of labels and of paths already plotted.

When a passion becomes a business

At the beginning there is Riccardo, a 23-year-old young man who is doing an internship at the marketing office of a company in Chicago, and one evening he buys from a US provider the domain on which his friend, Chiara Ferragni, intends to publish her first post of *The Blonde Salad*.

Just three years later, the two are invited to present their experience to the students at Harvard. And this is only the beginning of a rise that will lead them to build a company with a turnover of millions of euros – but it is, above all, a project so innovative as to become one of the pinnacles of the profound change in the fashion system rules at an international level.

Today, at just over 30 years old, Riccardo Pozzoli has a series of avant-garde entrepreneurial initiatives in the fields of fashion, food, lifestyle and social media behind him: a story of courage, creativity and passion thanks to which we can interpret our time with a new perspective.

Pozzoli's view on the present and future frontiers of business is encouraging without taking any prisoners, pragmatic without ever losing vision and poetry, very easy to read and yet very rich in information and ideas.

Together with him we will find out who really is a startupper. We will learn how to turn a dream into a precise idea, and an idea into a company. What to do in practice when you start from scratch, and you need courage and tenacity to give substance to a project yet to be built. How to start again when life forces us – or desire forces us – to turn over a new page, building on successes as well as failures.

Acknowledgements

This book is the result of years of professional (and not only) experience, so I should thank every single individual who has contributed to this path, but it would take another book to do that and, alas, it is not feasible.

A heartfelt thanks goes to the incredible teams that have accompanied me and that still accompany me in these wonderful adventures: thanks to the TBS team that was and is, the Depop team, the Condé Nast team and the Foorban dream team!

If I had to choose, I would certainly like to start by giving thanks to the wonderful DeA group: Annachiara and Angela, who have accompanied me from conception to the present day; Enrica, with whom I have spent more time in the last six months than my wife; Riccardo and Raffaella, who helped me to organize the promotion. Thank you very much for always believing in me and for allowing me to carry out a beautiful project, once again with a great team!

Another huge thank you goes to the authors of the contributions, not only for the contributions themselves (exceptional!) but also and above all for having been my mentors during so many stages, and having taught, spurred, inspired and fascinated me. So thanks (in order of appearance) to Lorenzo, Simon, Max, Matteo, Emanuela, Chiara, Luciano and Pierre-Yves!

The customary thanks to family is normal, but mine is really heartfelt, because without my mother's initiative and determination and my father's independence and ability to reinvent himself, I would probably have had very little experience, so thank you!

Last but not least, thanks goes to my beautiful wife, Gabrielle, who with her incredible energy helped me to overcome even the most difficult moments, and who with her enormous patience never told me to get lost after the endless days spent creating this book.

Introduction

*How to explain what you do for a living
to your neighbour*

Riccardo, what is it that you do for a living? Every time I am asked this question, I feel uncomfortable, especially if the person in front of me would like to hear a simple and reassuring answer such as: 'After graduating in economics, I took a job in the marketing department of a multinational company'. So, I mentally review all the answers I could give and despondently discard them one by one: 'consultant', 'speaker', 'serial startupper'... And then, to get out of the predicament, I tell a story.

It was October 2009, I was 23 years old and I was doing an internship in Chicago in the marketing department of a leading company in the production of irrigation products for gardens, terraces, kitchen gardens, and indoor and outdoor plants.

The university had recommended that opportunity to me and I thought it was interesting. I had never had a garden in my life and I barely knew what an irrigator was, but I told myself that it was worth trying: at least I would learn something new and live in a city where I had never been before for a few months.

I spent the first 15 days of the internship in the company's garden trying out all the products, then I went back to the office and started analysing the specialist blogs and literature posted on the internet by the companies in the sector. Two realizations began to dawn on me at that point. The first was that office work was not for me because I struggled to understand the purpose of all the rules and procedures imposed by the company and that, as I saw it, slowed down thinking, held back action and dampened the passion of even the most willing worker. The second was that in the United States, bloggers set trends and hugely influence consumption.

At the time I knew Chiara, a girl from Cremona who loved posting daily photographs of her different outfits and looks on social platforms such as Netlog, Flickr and Lookbook.nu, gathering a big following. So, we started talking about the possibility of Chiara starting her own blog about fashion and style. I saw a business opportunity in it, and although of course I did not yet know where it would lead us, I thought it was worth exploring. I bought the domain from a US provider and on 12 October, with the publication of the first post, *The Blonde Salad* was born.

At this point, I usually try to summarize everything that happened afterwards and the incredible adventure I experienced with the birth of the TBS Crew and the Chiara Ferragni Collection.

In the meantime, I have launched many other projects, some still in the field of fashion, others in completely different sectors, such as the Foorban food delivery service. Not all of them did well, but I never stopped trying. And above all, I never stopped.

In all of this I am aware that I have not answered my inquisitor's question, who after all only wanted to stick a reassuring label on me and put me in a specific category, something that many people find almost indispensable. This is an understandable need, but the point is precisely this: today that label is no longer as widespread nor as clear-cut as it used to be. And that is not just for those of us who, like me, are operating in the world of start-ups. We know very well how difficult it is for a working enterprise, whether as an entrepreneurial experience or as an employee, to fit within the boundaries of a professional life.

However, I would like everyone – from students who are entering the world of work, to workers who have to deal with uncertainty and the end of steady jobs, to 40- or 50-year-olds who, by their own will or necessity, are having to reinvent themselves at an age when it would previously have been considered impossible to do so – to try to think not only of the disadvantages but also of the opportunities that such a situation offers. Paths open up in front of us these days and we have no idea where they may lead. Today we have the possibility of turning what look like unmarked tracks into four-lane motorways.

I do not want to hide the difficulties of this type of enterprise and the sacrifices it requires; neither do I want to underestimate how high the risk of failure is, because I experienced all of this myself. The quid pro quo, however, is the opportunity to work with passion and build a more rewarding reality around yourself: now is the time to try.

Today we have the possibility of turning what look like unmarked tracks into four-lane motorways.

For those who want to take on a venture and create a startup as I did, there is the advantage of being able to raise capital more easily than before, because, as I shall explain, the financial crisis in 2007–08 at least offered this as a positive consequence. But it is not compulsory to create companies from scratch: you can also innovate from within using what already exists and using the new tools at our disposal.

The neighbour, the uncle, the high school teacher, all those who have loved us since we were children and want to be reassured about our future, must accept it. For our generation it is natural to have more than one important love story and to undertake more than one professional project in the course of our lives. This does not mean that we are less inclined to commit ourselves. It just means that our reality is less stable than it once was. And maybe even that we are less willing to settle for less – in addition to working, we also want to feel fulfilled.

Where the labels stop, the new world begins. And I think happiness begins too.

The story of *The Blonde Salad*

October 2009: With the publication of the first post on 12 October 2009, *The Blonde Salad* blog is born. The posts revolve around Chiara Ferragni's various interests: fashion first and foremost, and then photography, travel and lifestyle. The fact that they are published every day at the same time, 9 o'clock in the morning, makes reading the blog a daily habit for many followers. After the first month, in fact, *The Blonde Salad* is already recording 30,000 daily visits.

February 2010: After only three months from the birth of the blog, Chiara Ferragni is invited for the first time to the Milan Fashion Week. The presence of a fashion blogger is an absolute novelty, and this attracts the attention of the press and various brands such as Benetton, which offers her the role as judge of an online competition for the brand's new advertising campaign, and Fiat, which sponsors a trip around Europe in a Fiat 500 convertible for Chiara and Riccardo. Meanwhile, Yoox, a leading online fashion retailer, is one of the first to buy publicity banners on *The Blonde Salad*.

March 2011: Chiara and Riccardo set up TBS Crew. The blog has now reached 70,000 daily visits, and various luxury brands that are beginning to appear in the online sales market and are looking for ways to increase them, offer them collaborations. The two entrepreneurs are very selective in their choice of partnerships, stimulated as they are by the desire not to render the blog a simple showcase for purchases, but instead to offer readers content consistent with Chiara's image and to build lasting relationships with the various brands, especially the luxury ones.

March 2013: Chiara is now an international celebrity. She appears on the covers of fashion magazines all over the world and continues to collaborate with important brands, for which she also creates capsule collections. Her popularity is also growing thanks to Instagram. Meanwhile Chiara, Riccardo, the investor Paolo Barletta and the sales manager Lorenzo Barindelli found a new company, the Chiara Ferragni Collection, which produces and markets a line of shoes that are sold online and in 200 shops in 25 countries.

First months of 2014: *The Blonde Salad* website is completely reorganized, becoming a real lifestyle magazine, collaborating with the best photographers and video makers. The team is also invited by the MBA professors at the Harvard Business School, who had chosen *The Blonde Salad* as a case study for their students.

September 2016: *The Blonde Salad* changes again, enriching itself with a new e-commerce section, where limited editions created exclusively by international brands are sold. This new initiative is also welcomed with enthusiasm by followers: the items proposed are systematically sold out within hours.

July 2017: The Chiara Ferragni Collection opens its first flagship store in Milan. The collection now also includes accessories and clothing.

September 2017: Chiara, with over 11 million followers on Instagram, is crowned the most important fashion influencer in the world by *Forbes* magazine.

CHAPTER ONE

Instructions on how to get outside the box

- *Obstacles, mental moulds and opportunities in the world of work today.*

There is a huge crisis

What bad luck it is to live in the decade following one of the worst economic crises in history, huh? That is what we are used to thinking.

Undoubtedly, in recent years a great many things have changed and the world of work has been hit by profound transformations. Young people who complete their studies know that their professional development will not be established from the outset and be almost 'fixed' as it once was. They know too that, unlike in the past, it is not certain they will do the same job for life, because the steady job no longer exists. In the course of your career it is all too likely that you will change roles, sectors and even type of work, whether as an employee or as a self-employed person. All this uncertainty can be frightening. When the mould breaks, understanding your place in the world is more difficult and less automatic.

Since focusing on the negative aspects is of no use, and certainly does not change a working reality that is profoundly different from the one that others faced 30 years ago, it is better to shake off the pessimism and understand that the end of the era of labels and plotted paths can also be extremely liberating. Not having to necessarily fit into a predefined mould, in fact, means being free to explore and eventually build yourself a more rewarding professional path. That sense of security that changing working conditions force us to give up, can be bartered for (more) important things such as freedom, happiness and passion for what we do.

Not having to fit into a predefined mould means being free to explore.

We must also bear in mind that in recent years we have not just been subjected to a flurry of bad luck but have also had many possibilities open up before us, because the digital revolution has created new and potentially endless business opportunities. Thanks to technological innovations now available to everyone, new jobs are being invented. Even extremely traditional roles can be rethought in a completely different way, and a much wider market can be accessed whose boundaries are potentially limitless.

Freeing oneself from beliefs, attitudes and positions

Even though I am an optimist, I do not want to make the mistake of painting the current world of work as a mythical Eldorado, because that would be equally misleading. I just think that there are opportunities for those who are not afraid to change and do not cling onto the status quo tooth and nail, who are willing to work hard and are able to seize those opportunities.

To do this, you must first be able to think outside the box, to be in the habit of observing the problem from different angles. It is a skill that everyone can develop or refine but which is generally more associated with a 'lateral' position than a specific sector. In other words, when you are already in a particular context, it is easier to be conditioned by your previous experiences and, therefore, find it more difficult to innovate. If you have a family business that has followed certain rules for years, decades, it is more difficult to have the insight to change things and improve them. It is inevitable that a background, a previous training, will bring with it a series of prejudices that are the sworn enemies of open-mindedness.

There are opportunities for those who are not afraid to change.

I have often discussed these issues with my friends Stefano Cavaleri and Marco Mottolese, with whom I founded a lunch delivery service called Foorban at the beginning of 2016. For the moment it is the only one available in Milan, but we plan to launch in other European cities, given its success – a success that depends on the quality and uniqueness of the service offered (a concept that I will return to). Foorban's distinguishing feature is to deliver very quickly – thus meeting the needs of workers on their lunch break – tasty and healthy dishes that are prepared in our exclusive kitchen rather than by various restaurants, as is the case with other companies that offer food delivery. To all intents and purposes, Foorban is a restaurant whose place settings are scattered throughout the city and not confined to a single place!

My associates and I have wondered if a reality like ours could have come from the mind of a restaurateur. The answer we have come to so far is 'no', because when you are in a certain sector it is difficult to see it in any other way than the traditional one. Between myself, Stefano and Marco, only the last had experience in the field. After he graduated in economics, he worked in the field of catering for large events and then opened a restaurant in Milan. So you could say that the guys and I saw catering from the outside and this allowed us to invent something new.

Obviously, this does not mean that it is completely impossible to break out of the mould while remaining in the sector in which you have always worked or in which your family works. In fact, there are those who do not allow themselves to be restrained by their own or their family history, and indeed use it as a starting point to change everything, exploring the possibilities that current reality provides us with.

This is the case with one of our Foorban suppliers – Andrea Passanisi, the creator of Sicily Avocado. After a trip to Brazil, he conceived of the idea of growing subtropical fruit on the slopes of Mount Etna, following in the footsteps of his grandfather, an agricultural entrepreneur, and converting land that had always been cultivated for lemons to the production of avocados. The idea has proved to be successful. The microclimate of the area makes for an excellent product from an organoleptic point of view, which is now exported and appreciated throughout Europe... and sold to customers online.

There are many stories like this, because with an innovative approach even very traditional sectors can offer business opportunities. You can start with something that already exists and give it a completely different shape to enable it to go much further.

With an innovative approach even very traditional sectors can offer business opportunities.

This is what my friend and fellow university graduate Fabio Di Gioia did. After working for a few years in the financial sector, he and a partner launched a startup company called Foodscovery. It is a platform that brings together local producers and lovers of gastronomic refinement, who can order Chianina meat, mozzarella from Campania, *taralli* from Puglia and all the other delicacies of the Italian agri-food industry and have them delivered fresh quickly. The work of the Foodscovery team consists primarily in finding these typical products of the highest quality and presenting and enhancing them appropriately on their website. So they had to devise a very simple system, based on SMS technology, to allow even those artisans who were not as familiar with smartphones and computers to receive orders quickly and clearly. Then they made sure the courier delivered the order to the final customer in the shortest possible time. Fabio and his partner have managed to secure agreements with the main couriers to deliver *cannoli* from Sicily and *pasticciotti* pastries from Puglia throughout Europe inside 48 hours. Their platform differs from all the others operating in this sector because it allows customers to buy not only typical products in cans or vacuum-packed but also very fresh and perishable foods, such as the Neapolitan cake, the *pastiera*.

Exploiting the great artisan traditions of Italy and making them available to a wider public and market is one possible opportunity, but there are so many more. The essential thing is to have the open-mindedness to spot the opportunities and the curiosity to look further into them and understand whether or not they will be practicable.

The experience of Foorban is an example of how, even the most traditional sector, that of catering, can be interpreted in a completely different way thanks to new technologies that allow you to meet the needs of customers in new and unexplored ways. And this applies to any sector: sport, for example, or anything related to travel, where incredibly there is still little development. Another almost virgin area is the design sector – considering that some of the companies involved in this field often do not even use social media channels to communicate with potential customers, the room for manoeuvre is really very wide.

In any case, regardless of the sector, I think the most important thing is to take note of the fact that this is the environment now. Wearing blinkers, pretending not to see change, or even opposing it, is at the very least a risky decision. It makes me think of the world of publishing, which, in the face of digital progress, has suffered from neophobia. The fear of the new and of change has prevented publishers from exploiting their position of advantage and monopolizing the digital sector. This has affected many companies that, after initially rejecting such technologies, are now finding themselves having to run along to keep up with the changes instead of riding with them as they could have done had they not remained so entrenched in their conservative ways.

Having the courage to think big

Doing business today, however, does not necessarily mean you need to be a 'geek' and have to design apps or websites. Even in a digitalized age like ours, innovative projects can arise outside of the technological field.

Doing business today does not necessarily mean you need to be a 'geek' and have to design apps or websites.

This is the case of the project started by three of my Italian friends who have been living in the United States for some years now, Francesco Brachetti, Alberto Gramigni and Alessandro Biggi. They opened the first restaurant in the world dedicated exclusively to the avocado. It is called Avocaderia and is in Brooklyn. The idea was very popular and had an extraordinary media response even before the opening. The venue attracts thousands of customers every week, and the team continues expanding, opening more venues for now in Manhattan and soon in California. What made the difference in their case, in addition to the idea – which was in tune with one of the food trends of the moment – and the quality of what they prepare, was the audacity to immediately think big, not just of a simple restaurant but of a real enterprise that could turn into a chain of avocado bars. The fact that the product is good and that customers like it so much is enabling them to make that happen.

So, knowing how to think big is another fundamental characteristic for success in the world of work. This is what Max Ciociola has. He founded Musixmatch, one of the most successful Italian startups. His idea was also mentioned by Mark Zuckerberg, the creator of Facebook, as a winning example to follow in a recent speech. Musixmatch – accessible as a website and smartphone app – offers the largest online catalogue of song lyrics and now has more than 60 million users. Musixmatch was born of a very definite need for Max who, besides being an engineer, is a passionate musician and therefore always wanted to have to hand the lyrics of the songs he listened to or played. Max imagined that he could not be the only person to want this, and so he thought of creating an app that would allow you to view the lyrics of the song you are listening to on the device that is playing the music, for example your smartphone.

It is an ingeniously simple idea that has made life easier for millions of music lovers around the world. Max was also brilliant because, unlike many before him, he understood that it would not be possible to create such an app without paying the record companies for the rights. He understood the value of the works of genius, which the songs were, and that they ought to be recognized and paid for. He therefore sought sufficient investment to pay for the royalties, carry out marketing that would allow him to reach at least 1 million users in the first instance and, of course, to cover any development costs. We are talking big figures, but having the certainty of being able to reach such a high number of users also gave him the certainty of being able to sell the advertising well. With a

You have to have the courage and the bravery to think big.

large initial investment, he was able to pay the royalties and start big: from then on, the mechanism was self-sufficient.

Max's story teaches us that we must have the courage and perhaps even the bravery to think big: if he had decided to start quietly, without an agreement with the record companies, which was very expensive, he would probably have been forced to close down after three months, and his idea, however valid, would have died there and then.

Perseverance, patience and passion

Of course, visionary enthusiasm must be balanced by a good dose of reality, because at the beginning it is important to proceed carefully. But setting a target that is not too easily achievable can provide the impetus to secure a great result. When you start from scratch with a new idea, you have to be very patient and not let the first difficulties defeat you, because there is no certainty that things will happen within the timeframe you first thought of. It is possible that for the first six months nothing will happen, and then it will suddenly explode. To patience I add another very important skill: perseverance, the ability to hold on and not give up. If you have an idea, a project, a dream, but you are not determined enough to pursue it, then there is no point in having it.

If you have an idea, a project, a dream, but you are not determined enough to pursue it, then there is no point in having it.

The beautiful thing about our era is that, unlike what has happened in the past, the place where you were born or the family environment you came from are no longer so important in forming you as a person. Reading, learning, travelling, coming into contact with different realities are no longer the exclusive prerogative of only certain social groups.

I am reminded of the case of Jeremy Scott, the creative director of Moschino, who is one of the most famous and acclaimed designers of the moment and is also one of the pop icons of our time, regardless of how you judge his creations, which are eclectic and unexpected to say the least. Scott was born and raised in a context that had nothing to do with fashion, in a small town in Missouri, to a middle-class family. He is proof that if you have a dream, if you believe in something, if you have passion and you work hard, then you can get there.

Of course, you need to have the desire and curiosity to grasp these stimuli and the open-mindedness to be influenced by them, knowing that they are essential in all phases of the conception and implementation of a project and not just the initial one.

At the end of 2015 I was in Bologna visiting the Musixmatch offices. I was walking around the city with my phone attached to my ear. On the other side of the screen were Marco and Stefano, and together we were trying to find a name for the lunch delivery service that we had been working on for some time now. It was a real brainstorming session, where everyone put some ideas on the table, hoping that at some point the right one would jump out. Initially the name we had thought of was Food-bowl, referring to the fashion of using bowls – salad bowls and bowls full of vegetables, grains and proteins, seasoned with sauces and various seeds – that was spreading in the United States and, from there, all over the world. However, we realized that the name sounded too much like 'football' and that it would therefore be misleading, because it would make people think of the sport, which had nothing to do with our bowls. So we put everything back on the table and thought again about the fundamental concepts of the business we were developing: on the one hand, food, of course, and on the other, the city, the extremely dynamic urban context we wanted to turn to. So, from the fusion of 'food' and 'urban', the name of our startup popped up: Foorban. What does this have to do with the fact that I was in Bologna visiting Musixmatch? Well, I am sure it inspired me. Not directly, of course, but stimuli are almost never direct... and that is something I learnt in high school, studying Latin, which greatly shaped my way of thinking, giving me an analytical approach. In the same way, I believe that meeting someone as brilliant as Max and visiting his company that day stimulated me to find the right approach to creating the name for our business.

Of course, it does not always happen that way and not all ideas that come to mind are necessarily going to be the right ones or achievable. My partners and I did many of these brainstorming sessions during the ideation phase for Foorban. Most of them were held at Tom, Marco's restaurant in Milan. At that time we spent whole days there working on our project and, when the restaurant was closed, the chefs also used us as guinea pigs, making us try out new dishes they intended to include on the menu. Their experiments were not always successful, just as not all our ideas were usable... but the important thing was to try and not give up. This is true both when you cook and when you have a business project!

Studying is not about filling a bucket, it is about lighting a fire

With regards to Latin and how my studies have influenced my way of thinking, I must say that I am very happy to have attended the school I did: a tough state scientific high school in Busto Arsizio, with an experimental programme that gave a lot of space to the study of languages and literature (Italian, Latin, English and French) at the expense of hours of mathematics. I am a great advocate of Latin and I do not understand those who say that studying it is a waste of time, just because it is not something you use every day. It is certainly true that Latin is not used every day, but the mind is certainly used every day... and Latin moulds it, it teaches you a way of reasoning that in life is more useful than many practical notions. Obviously to stay in the world of work you have to fill that gap between theory and practice sooner or later, because it is true that those who come out of high school know how to create a Latin translation, but not an invoice. However, I am convinced that there is always time to learn practical things: through studies it is more important to acquire a valid mindset.

And anyway, speaking of studies, my experience has taught me that anything is possible. I have friends who did very badly in high school and started successful businesses as soon as they left school, and I have others who followed a 'normal' educational path, graduated in finance with honours, worked in investment banks until they were 30, going around Europe and the rest of the world, to then return to Italy and become entrepreneurs.

After all, the most important thing in business is to have a great desire to work, and you cannot teach that. But it is also true that there are courses of study that can help you learn how to launch a company.

I am happy with the educational course I have followed, first graduating in finance and then doing a master's degree in marketing. What I like about it is that they are disciplines that are in some ways antithetical – finance has a scientific, numerical approach and therefore teaches an analytical method, while marketing is made up above all of intuition, of a sensitivity that is not necessarily related to economic analysis.

Finance has also taught me how to evaluate a company or a company asset, which today is very useful to me because, when I go to ask investors for finance for my projects, I can evaluate my company following clear mechanisms, and this helps me to present it better. Of course, if I had not studied finance, I would have learned about it – the fact of knowing about finance, of having studied it, did not change my life, but it has helped me a lot.

The master's degree in marketing, on the other hand, taught me sectoral reasoning, so much so that at the basis of all my reasoning there are the variables that traditionally constitute the 'marketing mix', that is, the so-called '4Ps': product, price, place, promotion. It is a classic concept, but it is what guided me, for example, in the very early stages of creating *The Blonde Salad* when I was trying to apply what I was learning to what we were beginning to create.

For this reason I think that an education in marketing is of great interest. But I am talking about pure marketing, not about those courses focused only on communication. Often, in fact, the word 'marketing' is confused with simple promotion, whereas preparing something for the market means working on all the decision-making levers: product, price, place and promotion. Obviously, when you start with a whole new project, knowing how to make it attractive to the market is of great interest.

In this case too, clearly the entrepreneurial style of each person is decisive. I am a man of marketing and therefore I tend to have a more creative approach than a financial one. This in itself is neither a good nor a bad thing for a company. If my approach had been different, more oriented to finance, maybe I would not have needed a finance director but rather a very creative marketing director.

It is clear that, in the startup phase of a company, having ideas on how to ensure that it works well for customers is a priority over the fact that it works well economically, because at the beginning only you can know your idea and how you want to sell it to the world, while it is easier to find someone who can help you with the financial framework of the company. Then, as the company grows over time, having strong financial skills becomes more and more important.

In general, I would say that today, for those who are planning to launch their own business, sector studies are limiting. I started in the world of fashion, then I began to take an interest in catering and maybe in the future I will want to work in other, completely different fields. Nowadays this is not unusual, and it is the reason why I believe a vertical grounding, in only one sector, is a little counterproductive. If you want to do business in the field of design, for example, it is pointless learning everything you need to know about design at the beginning, because maybe your idea will not work and therefore you will need to change direction. It is much better to have a less sectorial approach that, instead, helps us to manage the launch of something, or that allows us to manage a company. It should also be borne in mind that usually, when you attend degree courses in management and marketing, the business cases you study are mostly multinationals, so, when you start from scratch with a project, things are very different from the theory and you will have a lot to learn on the job. As in all aspects of life, you learn by doing and by making mistakes!

Then there is always the case of those who manage to launch a successful business without any university education. And this is because being an entrepreneur is something that you have inside you: certainly studies can be useful, but so too can work and personal experiences, such as travel or comparison with others. What you really need is to have a mental approach that allows you to identify needs, understand problems, address them and find the right solutions, building something. This is what allows you to do business in any industry and at any time. An intelligent and capable person will be able to take what is really important from every course of study, and more generally from every experience, discarding what is of no use. And so any course of study can be more or less useful, while entrepreneurial thinking and mindset are difficult to teach.

In the end, however, I believe that all these personal characteristics – the open-mindedness needed to think outside the

What is really needed is a mental approach that allows you to identify needs, understand problems and find the right solutions.

box, curiosity, daring, patience, perseverance – and also everything you can learn through study and experience are useless if there is no passion for what you do, which is the most important thing of all. When you start a project, in fact, you are usually alone, or at least there are just a few of you; you work a lot, you have to constantly make a lot of effort, there are many sacrifices to bear and the gains may be few or non-existent. But if it is something you are passionate about, work becomes a wonderful thing. Not a constraint, but the reason why you get up in the morning.

CHAPTER TWO

Start...up! Start and start again

- *What is a startup?*
- *What it takes to start and start again.*

Don't shoot the startupper

I know, most people get irritated when they hear about startups. This is because, especially in Italy, a somewhat simplistic and ridiculous rhetoric has taken hold that brings to mind an image of kids who become millionaires in a few months thanks to a winning idea, young Ted Talk gurus, or nerds locked inside a garage working on obscure algorithms to invent the next app.

In reality, this abused term simply indicates the startup phase of a new company, with all that it entails at an organizational and structural level. In addition, the term startup is often confused with the design of apps or with the launch of solely internet-based projects. In reality, while it is true that in its original definition the concept of startups referred to a specific type of business, characterized by a strong digital matrix and able to offer absolute cutting-edge solutions, over time this definition has become more flexible and has come to include newly founded companies operating in the most diverse sectors. The startup, therefore, is a rather broad concept and can also mean launching a new project within a corporate group, like a spinoff, a rib that detaches itself from the parent company to develop collateral businesses.

These new-born companies usually have one or more founders and one or more financiers. It is a model, borrowed from US startups, that is extremely innovative for a country like Italy, because in this case you do not need to have an initial capital set aside to found a company. The founder has an idea, builds a business plan and finds the money to set up his or her company. It is a much more democratic model than the classic idea according to which only those who already have the initial capital put aside, perhaps because they are from a rich family (the classic rich kid, for instance), can set up a company.

One in a thousand makes it

Obviously this does not mean that it is easy to start and it is even less easy to survive: in the first 18 to 30 months of existence – which is what it generally takes to move out of the startup phase – a company faces the harsh reality of the world and the market, and it is possible, I would even say probable, that it may suffer a bloody nose. At the beginning, a startup is like a gazelle that has to run for its life. You cannot make any mistakes, because the competition is really tough.

It is estimated that in Italy two startups in 10 shut down within the first three years. There are many reasons why this happens – some startups simply cannot keep up with the competition;

others do not have a sustainable business model; still others fail because of the inadequacy of the product, the depletion of cash or because of legal issues. I know this statistic may seem negative and discouraging, but in all honesty, it looks good to me!

Unfortunately in Italy it is often difficult to see it like this, because it is part of our entrepreneurial culture to want everything immediately, almost as if we could start a company today and become millionaires

At the beginning, a startup is like a gazelle that has to run for its life.

tomorrow. It does not actually work that way, especially nowadays, when the potential market is bigger but there is also much fiercer competition. So those thinking of jumping into this field must be ready to roll up their sleeves, be aware that the risk of failure is high and that it may take longer than expected to achieve the goals set.

In any case, it seems to me an extraordinary innovation that those who have an idea but no capital can at least try to access funding to make it a reality.

It must be said that the startup method is a way of doing business that in Italy still remains largely unexplored, precisely because we are lagging behind the United States and other European countries such as the UK and France. In a structured economy like ours, startups still carry little weight. Of course, the fact that we are getting there is a good sign, but you must also keep in mind that traditionally the Italian investor / saver is one of the most conservative figures and has a really low tolerance of risk. This indisputable reality has some positive aspects, because it is what, for example, has allowed the Italian financial system to never fail, but it inevitably clashes with the startup method, which requires investors to be more inclined to risk. After all, the 'venture' in 'venture capitalist' means 'adventure' and this immediately suggests that the risk rate is very high. If I were to open my own small investment fund tomorrow, I would invest in 10 startups with the idea that one would do very well, three would do so-so, and six would fail. This is more or less the risk you have to be willing to take.

I also think it is important to point out that another obstacle is the range of vision of Italian entrepreneurs. It is not only investors but also entrepreneurs who have difficulty thinking big, because we are a little reserved in our way of doing business. It is no coincidence that the largest Italian companies were built 50 years ago and not today. We are a country of small- and medium-sized enterprises. Therefore, even in the case of startups, we set out with the idea of creating a small- or medium-sized business and therefore we make small- and medium-sized investments, when instead the most interesting opportunities arise when we are able to aim high.

This reserved attitude is counterproductive, because the startup must not only be functional and operational but also interesting from a financial point of view. The priority is to work well and be attractive to customers, of course, but also to maintain a level of appeal to investors as well. And to achieve this, in my opinion, you have to think big, sell yourself to investors with a clear idea of what you want to do and not be afraid to be daring in terms of the size of your business.

The sky above Roncade

Having said that, I would also like to point out that in this historical period it is not so difficult to find money, even in our country, because there is greater liquidity now than there has been since the end of the war. The financial crisis of 2007–08 in fact provoked an enormous fear of traditional investments – investors dismantled capital, selling bonds and shares, and repatriating liquidity, which they now have to manage in a different way from investment in the financial markets.

Banks have liquidity but also a whole series of investment funds, entrepreneurs and so-called *angel investors*, that is people who have resources to invest. They are all people who do not know what to do with this liquidity, precisely because the stock exchange has investments that are too risky, and therefore they are becoming increasingly interested in investing in startups, often in exchange for equity. This is why venture capital funds, small funds or investment groups of small entrepreneurs are emerging, that is to say countless more or less institutional intermediaries who have the capital and are willing to invest it, even on young people, because they are used to having slightly higher risk profiles.

Usually a startup goes through several investment phases. Generally they start with seed capital, which is the first level of financial funding that is accessed to launch a new business. Seed capital is almost always scraped together from various angel investors. My partners and I did just that with Foorban – a first phase of seed capital with investors who gave us variable amounts, collecting a total of 500,000 euros. Then we undertook a few further rounds of seed funding that generated a total of four million euros.

After this phase, you move onto securing more substantial investment, turning not to angel investors, but to venture capitalists.

Sometimes, however, a startup goes through an incubation phase. Business incubators are realities created specifically for startups that have not yet officially started a business or are at a very early stage. The incubator investors take them almost literally by the hand and invest skills, time, contacts, offices and economic resources to encourage their development, in exchange for company shares, which makes them in effect active partners in the process of the creation and development of the project. That is, they help the startupper to deal with the phase of 'from zero to one' and, rather than providing capital, they offer the network and know-how to make the idea ready to go live. They provide fiscal, legal and organizational support as well as, often, assistance in terms of strategy and marketing. And, when they think the time has come, they accompany the startupper to meet the Italian or international venture capitalist.

One of the main Italian incubators, H-Farm, helped my friend, Simon Beckerman – a Milanese with a British father – to create Depop, a social shopping app that allows everyone to buy and sell directly from their smartphones. It was founded in 2010 and today it is one of the most prestigious companies on the mobile market, with more than 20 million users, 3 offices, in London, New York and Los Angeles, and a team of 120 employees. Depop is a highly active app that is exploding on the scene of European startups. It is a world I know well because I am a member of its advisory board, a group of industry experts that advise the executive team.

The history of Depop is fascinating and emblematic. Simon was 37 years old and had various professional experiences behind him when he decided to take a vacation period to think of a new project to devote himself to. In those months he did everything and anything and thought a lot, until one day he started drawing the interface of an app in a notebook that would allow him to shop online. Simon had always been a great collector of trainers and felt there were no sites that would allow someone to buy used items while offering a fun user experience. After about 10 attempts, he thought the idea could be interesting and sent an e-mail to H-Farm. They invited him to the Roncade office near Venice, and after listening to his idea they decided to help him, providing him with an office, a tutor to help him formulate a business plan and some money. The incubation period lasted six months, during which they started the project, developed the app and launched it on the App Store. Simon then flew to London, where he met the biggest venture capitalists, who then decided to finance the project. Depop is now worth more than 200 million pounds.

Simon is someone with the right mentality, who was not afraid to try and who was able to make great use of the resources provided by the incubator.

Of course, this is not the only way forward. There are other realities that offer a fair visibility to new projects, like showcases for startups and days organized by incubators such as H-Farm, Nana Bianca and many others, which allow startuppers to present their ideas to representatives of venture capital and private angels and which often conclude with investment.

Where to start?

The following is Italy-specific but, of course, entrepreneurs working in other countries will find similar information and help from local and other organizations.

A good starting point for collecting information on incubators, accelerators, showcases and competitions for startups in Italy is the website startupitalia.eu.

The article (in Italian) economyup.it/startup/acceleratori-e-incubatori-dove-andare-per-far-nascere-un-impresa contains a list of the main Italian incubators and accelerators divided by region and is accompanied by an indication of the sector of specialization.

If you are looking for an angel investor, you can present your project to Italian Angels for Growth (IAG), the largest business angel network in Italy (italianangels.net).

The main venture capital funds in Italy are: Innogest SGR, 360 Capital Partners, Principia SGR, United Ventures, P101, Panakès Partners, Primomiglio SGR, Vertis SGR, Invitalia Ventures, Intesa Sanpaolo + Quadrivio, and OltreVenture (Source: startupitalia. eu/59998-20160707-fondi-venture-capita-italia).

Eyes fixed on the same goal

Another option available to those who want to launch their project and who need capital is crowdfunding. With this system, the promoter of an economic, social, cultural or charitable initiative asks users, through an internet platform, for the sums of money necessary to support it. The most famous crowdfunding platforms are Kickstarter and IndieGoGo, but there are many more and they finance creative projects of all kinds – not only startups but also comics, video games, music and books.

This is a very interesting system, but it cannot be used for every type of project. The process involved in fact requires the project be described in the greatest detail before it actually exists, so it is not suitable for those sectors that live off the surprise factor, such as fashion, for example. And it is no good either if what you want to launch is easily replicable, because when an idea is not yet on the market it can be stolen, unless it is really difficult to copy for technical reasons. In short, for those who create brands with a strong 'aspirational' content, this system is not viable, while it can be used more easily by those who are able to design and produce functional objects that do not yet exist and that require specialist skills to be created. That is why it is a very good method for the whole tech sector.

An example of this is OLO, the low-cost 3D printer that can be used with a smartphone thanks to special photo-hardening polymeric resins, which solidify with the light emitted by the screen of the device. The creators, Pietro Gabriele and Filippo Moroni, presented their idea on Kickstarter, with an enormously successful campaign that reached its goal in just a few hours.

Settling accounts

During the launch of a project, money is needed and it is likely that in the early stages there will be no earnings.

Let me elaborate with an example. Let us assume that a person undertakes some fundraising to launch their business and secures money from an investor of, say, 200,000 euros. The business needs the funding because in the first year it won't make a profit. It has no revenue, only costs of 100,000 euros. Let us say that in the second year it has revenues of 50,000 euros and costs of 100,000, therefore it needs another 50,000 euros. In the third year it may also have revenues, and let us hypothesize that they amount to 300,000, but the costs have also risen to 350,000, because to grow it was necessary to invest. So there was a deficit of 100,000 euros in the first year, 50,000 in the second year and 50,000 in the third. That is why they started with 200,000 euros in funds: because they knew that in the first three years they would spend more or less 200,000 euros more than they earned. So in the first phase there is no profit – if you make 100,000 euros, but you have costs of 200,000, you have losses of 100,000. If, on the other hand, you are good enough to make a profit – which is really very difficult – it is all the more necessary to invest it in your own business.

That is why I believe that, in principle, it is not possible to start without money. But of course everything depends on the type of business you have in mind. From my own personal experience, I and my Foorban associates started with 500,000 euros, while for the Chiara Ferragni Collection we needed 400,000 because they were activities that required certain types of costs to get them off the ground. With the former it was necessary to think about the logistics, both for the preparation of the dishes and for their distribution, as well as the development of the app. In the latter, it was necessary to register the trademarks and start the production of the footwear. Everything was different with *The Blonde Salad*, because we started with a blog. I took the photos and kept contact with the companies, while Chiara edited the photos and wrote the contents of the blog. In that case the investment was really minimal – 10 euros to buy the domain and 500 for a reflex camera. But it was a completely different business.

In my opinion, in short, we need to abandon the mentality of, 'I prefer to go it alone, even if I struggle', which is typical of much entrepreneurship, because then, when you are drowning, the business fails. And I think that having oxygen is more important, even if it means giving away 20 per cent of the company, if the alternative is to risk being left with nothing. Having 80 per cent of a good thing is better than having 100 per cent of nothing!

And, on the subject of the 'self-sufficiency syndrome', I think it is absurd to complain that Italian entrepreneurs, when they are unable to raise capital in their own country, turn to foreign investors, given that the largest European investment funds are British, French and German. I do not see why an Italian entrepreneur – who creates a startup in Italy – should not accept money from foreign investors. He or she will always be an Italian entrepreneur, even if the money is British, French or German. Nationalism can be a major limiting factor.

We need to abandon the mentality of 'I prefer to go it alone, even if I struggle'.

I am reminded of an example that has completely different proportions, but which I think is nevertheless significant – it is that of Gucci, a historic Italian brand that in 2004 was purchased by the French group Kering in a takeover. At the time, many people were angry and thought it was a scandal, without perhaps considering that the French did not buy Gucci to sink it but to see it flourish. Kering maintained Gucci's Italian character, which is its hallmark, in all respects. Gucci is French owned, but the CEO is Italian, as is the creative director, and the main offices are located in Italy. In short, in this case, the French were very farsighted to invest in one of the most beautiful Italian companies and keep it Italian, because that is the way it should be. And the same goes for startups – what is the problem with taking money from abroad to try to start a company in one's own country?

LORENZO GUIDOTTI Partner and Wealth Management and Family Office Area Manager of Solutions Capital Management SIM SPA

When you go to an investor to apply for funding for your business, no matter how strong and innovative the idea behind it may be, it is essential to convey that you have the passion and energy to carry the project forward and to prove that the team is the right one to put what you have in mind into practice.

I accompanied Marco Mottolese, Riccardo Pozzoli and Stefano Cavaleri to the investors when they were looking for funding for Foorban: in this case it was vital to show the investors that Marco was the product expert, Riccardo the marketing and branding expert and Stefano the entrepreneur, all intent on embodying the soul of the project. Without an entrepreneurial approach of this kind, it would be very difficult to succeed.

And not all financial backers are the same, just as their money is not. This concept is generally embodied in the 'smart money' formula, which means that the funds obtained from investors are accompanied by the investors' know-how, skills, networks and much more. Therefore, it is better to turn to financiers linked to the sector in question, as they may have more ways of looking at the project and adding value to it, in addition to just providing monetary resources.

'Smart money' indicates the funds obtained from those who, in addition to having the money, also have the know-how and can bring skills, networks and much more to the project.

Among other things, it is essential to be able to bring in investment without diluting the business too much, without doing too many rounds and without losing control of the company. The intermediary has a fundamental role to play here as well. This is why I believe that, in the first instance, in the seed phase, it is better to turn to incubators or other entrepreneurs, the so-called angel investors, rather than to venture capitalists. It is easier for them to understand how important it is to leave control of the company to the founder so that it does not radically change. They also understand how premature it would be to start asking for KPIs (key performance indicators, i.e. the indices that monitor the progress of a company process) straight away. After all, just like an entrepreneur, the investor must also be able to follow his or her instinct, an indispensable quality to be able to put money into a project that is still in the early stages and which is often difficult to fully understand and predict in terms of its potential.

CHAPTER THREE

Have a vision (even) without being a seer

- *How to come up with an idea and turn it into a company.*
- *Outline a vision and give it substance.*
- *The idea alone is not enough.*

Dreaming with your eyes wide open

In the language of marketing, the term vision is used to indicate the idea that the entrepreneur has of his or her company, and it is the basis for any business plan. In other words, it is the projection of a future scenario that reflects the values and spirit of a company, and all decisions that are taken must be aimed at the realization of that scenario and be consistent with it.

For example, Twitter's vision statement reads, 'Give everyone the power to create and share ideas and information instantly, without barriers'. That of Google, 'To organize the world's information and make it universally accessible and useful'. That of Instagram, 'To capture and share the world's moments'.

When you least expect it

Why do some people have a vision and others do not? It is partly a question of character, but I would say that it depends above all on a set of variables that must come together: education, background and experiences.

It helps to have people around us who teach us to dream, who do not put limits on us, who do not influence us with their closed mindset. My parents did this for me, even though at the beginning of my experience with *The Blonde Salad* it was not easy for them to understand exactly what was happening, because they were unfamiliar with blogs, social media and so on. Of course, the first revenues came when I was still doing my degree dissertation, and this helped me to understand – and helped my family to understand – that we were going in the right direction and that there was a business opportunity. But it was certainly much more risky than a career in banking, which was the most immediate opportunity for those who like me had studied finance. But when I think about it again now, I realize that it was more my own worry; it was more my own fear that starting something that had nothing to do with my studies was a mistake. My parents, on the other hand, have always supported me. Of course, they did not hide the fact that they had some reservations, but they never heaped pointless fears onto me. After all, I am convinced that we would make many mistakes without the help of those who, questioning what we are doing, push us to reflect and understand that not all intuitions are right.

It is important to have people at your side capable of advising you, maybe even people who are far removed from what you are doing. Sometimes you can see that it is the right way, but others think it is the wrong one. Often, having to face someone else helps to test your true conviction without having to necessarily find the support and understanding of others or make them change their mind. Also, sometimes something may not be absolutely right, but it may be right for you, and this is what counts most and what in the end makes it right.

Join the dots

The ability to have a vision can be learned. In this sense it helps greatly to have many experiences, to not be always locked in your shell, and to get to know different realities.

As far as I am concerned, one of the things that has shaped my way of thinking the most has been moving house so often. I know it may sound crazy, but in reality, our house is one of the most important things in our minds, and in the pyramid of human needs it comes second *The ability to have a vision can be learned.* after food. It is the symbol of our roots, of our security. And by the time I was 31 years old, I had already moved house at least 15 times. This has accustomed me to thinking that it is not so impossible to change things, because if every time I have managed to abandon what is symbolically perceived as the core of each of us and to restart, then change is always possible.

And it is something that applies on a personal level, of course, but also on a work level. It is always possible to start again by taking a new path, starting a new project. To do that, you must not be afraid to change, to take risks and to dream. And you must also have the courage to put the barrier far enough ahead of you, because if you put it too close you may jump over it too easily and then it becomes a problem identifying and preparing all the next steps.

At the same time, however, you also need to be patient, because, as I have said, having a vision means seeing something that does not exist, that is in another time. Obviously, the length of time depends on many things, the main one being the type of project it is. If my dream is to make wine, I must be aware that it is an activity that physiologically requires a lot of time. And so then it also requires perseverance, so I do not give up before I have achieved my goal. The various motivational phrases that are served up everywhere have ended up becoming redundant and boring, but it is really essential never to give up, because if you have a vision, everything is possible. I am talking, however, about achievable dreams, for which there are no objectively insurmountable obstacles that do not depend on us overcoming them. Other than that, I am convinced that we are in a historical moment in which every dream can become a reality. Of course, it can take longer than expected, maybe even a lifetime, and you have to be willing to pay the price – because there is always a price to pay – but in the end you can get there.

Another practical element that, in my opinion, must be borne in mind is that the dynamics of your private life may come into conflict with your professional aspirations, and at that point it is up to you to choose what to do. At least once I have found myself in a situation where, in order to fulfil a business dream, I would have had to pay a very high price on a personal level… and I decided not to do so. But there is no one answer for everyone or for any one moment in your life.

As I said, having a vision is not something for everyone, even if you can train yourself to develop one. Andrea Lorini, who has been a close friend of mine for many years and is now the managing director of the Chiara Ferragni Collection, always tells me that he and I could work together for the rest of our lives, because I have vision while he balances the books. And I agree wholeheartedly because we complement each other perfectly. However, it is important that those who have the vision know how to shape it correctly and, once they have defined it, that everything they do is aimed at its realization. Outlining your own vision is the most difficult thing of all, because over time it can evolve, but it must never be distorted. If you suddenly change direction, in fact, all that has been done up to that moment will have simply been a waste of time, resources and energy.

A vision allows you to turn the idea into a company. But what allows us to arrive at an idea is sensitivity, curiosity, open-mindedness and, yes, even context. Living in a stimulating context that pushes you to exercise your creativity and be forever curious, is an undeniable advantage, but of course you need to have the right character traits to be able to grasp these stimuli and render them fruitful. Humans are naturally curious; they are explorers, travellers, connoisseurs, otherwise progress would not have been possible. Everyone has this ability to explore, because if one person has managed it, everyone else can too. It is just that not everyone has the courage, the ability or the mental freedom to extract it.

A vision allows you to turn the idea into a company.

When I thought of *The Blonde Salad*, I had a girlfriend who loved to photograph her looks and post them online. I understood the sense of what she was doing and, at that time, my job consisted of analysing specialist blogs every day and dealing with communication on the web. The field was different, because it was about gardening and not fashion, but after all I was already familiar with social media, because during my adolescence Badoo, Netlog and MSN were all the rage. I was already projected into those realities and so, at the right time, I saw all the subplots aligning perfectly – I saw the dots join up.

In my opinion, the 'dots' give you the background and life experiences, and these are things that you can obtain, because, if you want to, almost everyone has the chance to explore. I am aware that the economic situation at the outset has a certain importance, but I think that today it is less so than it once was.

Today there is the internet, you can become informed, you can read, and even travel has become more accessible. And when I talk about travelling, I do not mean going who knows where or doing who knows what; it is more about a mental attitude, about the ability to keep your mind open to stimuli, to different perspectives, to the point of view of others. We know full well that there are people who never go anywhere but who are much more open-minded than those who travel the world but are not yet ready to let their minds wander.

Once you are confronted with the dots, it is up to your personal sensibility to join them up. To have an idea means to join creativity with sensitivity. At that point you understand that there is only one way to join up all those dots and that one way is the initial input that, combined with the vision, can become something real.

To arrive at an idea, however, you have to put yourself in the right frame of mind. First of all, you cannot know in advance whether you naturally have it or not, so it makes no sense to say *a priori*, 'I'm not creative enough'. You need to put yourself in a position to become it – travel, open your mind, read, become informed, experiment, live. And the great thing is that this process has nothing mechanical, direct or linear about it.

To have an idea means to join creativity with sensitivity.

When I was asked to do my internship in Chicago, I did not know much about products for irrigation, but I said to myself, 'I'm going precisely because I don't know'. In reality even after that experience, I still understood very little about gardening, but my mind opened up in ways that would otherwise have been unthinkable, and this helped with the birth of *The Blonde Salad*.

I think that the fact there is no direct correlation between the stimulus and a new idea is a beautiful thing, because it means that inspiration can really come from where you least expect it.

The idea is not enough

When I happen to talk to aspiring startuppers, I realize they have fallen a little for the myth of a winning idea. While it is true that there must be an idea at the base of the creation of a new company, it is also true that it is now almost impossible to invent something new. What makes the difference is putting the idea into practice.

I think this is a more current, less naive and definitely more complex concept in the sense that an idea may be brilliant, but if it is the wrong time, placed in the wrong market, by the wrong team, it will not go anywhere. Just as there are less interesting ideas, but they are put into practice so well that they can achieve exceptional results. Rather than having the idea of the century, the real advantage is having the resilience to be able to put it into practice in the right way.

Rather than having the idea of the century, the real advantage is having the resilience to be able to put it into practice in the right way.

Thanks to the experiences I have had so far, I have realized that even potential investors see it that way and, rather than just evaluating the idea itself, they wonder if those in front of them are able to realize it. They generally do not care if it is a sensational novelty, or whether all the numbers add up, or if the business plan is perfect, because they invest in people. That is what happened to me, Stefano and Marco when we looked for investors for Foorban – they wanted to meet all three of us to see if we were really the right team to turn that idea into a business.

When they asked me where we got our inspiration from for Foorban, I felt a bit like laughing because we copied the business model of a New York startup called Maple... which failed dramatically in just two years! Maple arose from an idea from the famous restaurateur and entrepreneur David Chang and debuted in Manhattan in the summer of 2015, offering a high level of service with gourmet lunches cooked in a dedicated restaurant and delivered to the customer in a quarter of an hour. Maple was a huge success; they managed to make US $20 million sales in a year, but then they went bankrupt. The problem was that, in an attempt to win over the whole market, they had lowered the price of their dishes to US $9. Of course, it was an economically unsustainable decision. With a business like that, where the raw ingredients cost a lot more than those of competitors who offer a more standard product, and with the costs associated with delivery in an area like Manhattan, it was unthinkable to enter into a price struggle – they could not win. In fact, at the third round of financing, investors refused to continue to bankroll it.

Maple's story contains various lessons, such as that you need to have a correct positioning and understand exactly what your target audience is. It is clear that such a product should not be offered to the masses, but to those who are more sensitive to the quality and healthiness of the raw ingredients, are willing to spend a little more and have the ability to do so.

In my opinion, in any case, the most important lesson of all is this – an idea may be right, but afterwards you also have to do everything else right, because every stage of creating a new business has its own perils. And that is what I am going to try to tell you about in the next chapter.

SIMON BECKERMAN   Serial Startupper and Founder of Depop

I think that a successful company always starts from the union of a good idea with a team of people who are culturally close to it. I often see people with fantastic ideas, but in areas and fields where they have no experience. It is precisely experience in the field in which you want to embark on an entrepreneurial project that leads to the cultural growth necessary to be successful. Otherwise you end up creating wonderful and very efficient empty boxes, without having the slightest idea of how to fill them.

It is much easier to create success from an average idea but with a great team than the other way around... though of course the ideal is to be able to count on both elements. Depop, my latest adventure, was born precisely because, when it came into my mind, I thought, 'This is a fantastic idea and it will be successful because, given my experience with what this company will do, I am the perfect person to take it forward'. So I decided to go for it. When you have these two fundamental ingredients you can start the adventure... And the more attuned these two ingredients are to each other, the more natural the process of creation will be and the better the result. This for me comes when it clicks – that is, when, after a lot of work, you wake up one morning and, after taking a deep breath, you realize that the pistons in the engine work autonomously and that you only have to add petrol.

For me, that means having achieved stage one. But this is not the final destination, because next comes two, three, etc!

My advice, therefore, is not to start with an idea just because you think you know how to make a business plan, you know a lot about the process of fundraising or because you know everything about how Google works. In my opinion, it is essential to analyse an idea and ask yourself if you are the right person to realize it; if it is only the idea that makes you feel passionate or also the community that you are going to serve. Only in the second case, in my opinion, are you really ready to take off!

It is much easier to create success from an average idea but with a great team than the other way around.

What pushed me and still pushes me in my entrepreneurial activity is the desire to build something that makes me independent and that gives me the opportunity to help others to be independent. The common element between all the companies I have founded or co-founded is the desire to create something new by exploring new frontiers and, through them, to show myself and others that there is always a way to create something that adds value to what already exists. The process of creation is what gives me the enthusiasm to go on... and I am convinced that this is not only true for me.

When we are young, we are prevented from doing many things because they are wrong or dangerous. But every time you say no to a child, you are telling them that being curious is wrong and that they are in danger of hurting themselves. In reality, curiosity is what, as an adult, will lead us to learn and, as a result, to create new things. A child who grows up with so many 'no's' will not want to do anything when they grow up, because they will be afraid of everything. And it is this conviction that we need to shake off – it is okay to make mistakes, because you learn more from failures than from successes. The important thing is to leave fear at home so you can keep your mind open to receive the lessons we learn when we go out there and do things.

For me the best moment is always when I start to see that people use my products. While I observe them I think of all the days and nights I spent working on the business, the discussions and quarrels, the anxieties and labours that served to create what others are using in that moment and that they bought with their money, the result of their work. Seeing that someone has spontaneously decided to spend their money or time on something you have created is an incredible emotion.

> *It is curiosity that drives us to learn and then to create.*

I remember when Kanye West had his creative consultant, Virgil Abloh, contact me and my brother Daniel when we were selling the sunglasses brand we had created, Super Sunglasses, because he wanted to produce a line of sunglasses with us… and Kanye came out of the bedroom of his New York apartment with a box full of Supers, saying that he had bought them all, to unequivocally clarify his appreciation for our product!

However, nothing that happened with Depop would have been possible if I had not listened to someone who did not give me a break for days with her unsolicited advice – my mother. In the period when I was looking for funding, she continuously repeated to me: 'Simon, there is an interview in GQ with Renzo Rosso, in which he says he invested in a technology campus for startups called H-Farm. Read the article, it might be good for your idea'. I did not listen to her for days and in the meantime, I was racking my brains on how to find a solution to my problem. In the end, since she was tormenting me, I told her: 'All right, mamma, I'll read it', more to get her to leave me alone than anything else. And then H-Farm proved to be fundamental to the success of Depop! It is true that mothers are always right…

CHAPTER FOUR

A camp bed in the office in order to go from zero to one

- *How to act effectively in the startup phase.*
- *The importance of programming and improvisation.*
- *The overlap of work and private life.*

Agent 00...1

'From zero to one' is a formula designed and made famous by Peter Thiel, co-founder of PayPal and Palantir and financier of some of the most important startups in Silicon Valley, including Facebook, SpaceX and LinkedIn.

Thiel argues that 'progress can take one of two forms. Horizontal or extensive progress means copying things that work – going from 1 to n. Horizontal progress is easy to imagine, because we already know what it looks like. Vertical or intensive progress means doing new things – going from 0 to 1'.[1] And how long does it take to cover the distance in terms of time and effort between two such close numbers? Certainly more than you imagine!

First of all, before you can go from zero to one you may have to try four or five 'zeros', because the first experience may not go well straight away. At least that is how it was for me.

One of my 'zeros' was my very first entrepreneurial experience, which I tried in 2005 when I was in my second year of university, together with my friend Stefano Cavaleri. Our idea was to create a social network for all the economics students to facilitate the exchange of readings, advice, books, notes, work opportunities and so on.

Our network was called ymgup, an acronym that stood for 'Young Managers Go Up'.

To all intents and purposes it was a precursor to LinkedIn, with a focus on economics students who were a little different in the sense that they were generally more focused on the world of work and more likely to join such a network.

The project was born from our desire to be more involved in the university reality that surrounded us, to network, but also, more trivially, to have a site that could keep us informed about all the parties organized by the various economics faculties. With hindsight I can say that it was a good and rather innovative idea, but even then, we could see its potential.

So we started by finding a web developer, who was a friend of friends, and we entrusted him with the creation of the site. The latter, however, took more than six months, because we did not have a budget to pay him and so he only worked on it in his spare time. Once the site was ready, we realized that we were not able to promote it. It was 2006, I was 20 years old and had a very limited network of contacts. I didn't have the followers on social networks that I have today to let them know that I had launched a new site... and, to tell you the truth, Facebook had just been born and Instagram did not even exist!

I mean, having never done a 'from zero to one', I didn't know what I was doing. I didn't know how much time was needed; I didn't know how much money I needed; and I didn't know how to communicate with our social network and tell them about it. That is why, even though we had a good idea to start with, the project crashed and burned. Despite the outcome, however, it was an important experience, which taught me many things on both the theoretical and practical levels; for example, I learned to manage a programmer and to review all the graphics he sent me. For me, who was not familiar with the practical aspects, it was important training.

The startupper is a pioneer and therefore must be able to take risks without being afraid to jump.

I think that when you start a new project, the most constructive attitude is to say, 'I'll try. Then if it doesn't work, it doesn't matter, but at least I'll have gained some experience and next time I'll certainly make fewer mistakes'. The startupper is a pioneer and must therefore be able to take risks without being afraid to jump – and above all he or she must be able to do instead of talk.

A goal is a dream with a project

Pioneer yes, but not a kamikaze. Throwing yourself in a reckless way into a risky enterprise, totally disregarding the chances of success, is never a good idea. That is why I think it is essential to have an agenda, a business plan, an operational tactical plan to follow. But, if circumstances so require, it is equally important to be able to improvise and not to remain blindly attached to your original project.

The plan serves as a point of reference, but if reality suggests going in another direction, you must be ready to do so. If, for example, you have a commercial activity and after three years you realize that you have the opportunity to open a new store, when the plan was to do so after five years, there is nothing to stop you changing your plans. If the business plan was to open a store in Rome and instead the trend of the first year of activity suggests that it is better to open it in Turin, of course that is what you must do.

The important thing is to make sensible decisions, and that is also why you need to have a business plan – you need to have a clear direction in order to recognize when you perhaps should not follow it. If you do not have any points of reference, it is harder to know when to change direction.

If you do not have any points of reference, it is harder to know when to change direction.

The business plan is a key element even if you intend to submit your project to a potential investor. There are many ways to create a business plan and you can find lots of information and templates on the internet to help you.

A business plan is not just about numbers; it is a proper presentation. The first thing you need to do is explain who the team members are, because when you want to convince an investor you have to make sure he or she believes in the team that will be involved in the project. The second fundamental step is to illustrate the problem you want to address. When I have to do this, I always think of a very famous scene from *The Wolf of Wall Street* – which is not a movie I am fond of, by the way, unlike many of my former college friends who have a Facebook profile photo of Leonardo DiCaprio as Jordan Belfort. The movie, however, makes me feel uncomfortable, because it seems to mythicize a totally negative reality. Despite that, I love the pen scene. One of the ways Jordan tests a salesman's skills is by asking him to try to sell him his own pen. The one who is most successful is Brad, the best dealer in the area, who doesn't get lost in small talk trying to convince him that the pen is more beautiful or special than the others, but makes sure he needs it. 'Would you do me a favour and write your name down on that napkin for me?' 'I don't have a pen...' 'Exactly. Supply and demand my friend.' This lightning-quick exchange illustrates better than so many theoretical treatises one of the fundamental aspects of marketing, i.e. the requirement to create an urgent need in order to be ready to satisfy it.

At that point it is necessary to explain how you intend to respond to the need that has been illustrated, showing how the project works, what its strengths are, who the target audience is, in short, present the so-called value proposition, including everything that distinguishes the future business from others already present in the market. This aspect is closely linked to the next step, which consists of outlining the market landscape and serves to identify direct and indirect competitors and to give a more precise idea of how large the potential market is. If you are looking to obtain funding it may also be useful to illustrate the funding rounds made by competitors.

This step preludes the part about the actual figures: first of all you have to calculate the startup costs, i.e. the expenses that will have to be incurred even just to start the business. These expenses include legal expenses, trademark registration, development of the website and the app, to name just a few examples related to the world of digital startups, such as those I have launched so far.

Then you need to present the operating costs for the first two years, which include marketing activities, payments to the business developer, personal consultant, administrative consultant, employees, the CEO, the graphic designer... and payments for the server, rental and management of the office, maintenance, and so on. Such a detailed expenditure forecast is essential when seeking financing, because only in this way can you determine how much you need to ask for from your investors.

The investors are then informed of the value of the company on the basis of the estimated revenues for the following two to three years. In this case it would be appropriate to outline various possible scenarios, because you cannot be sure how the business will go. The ideal is to propose three scenarios: a very pessimistic one, a reasonably realistic one and a very optimistic one.

The entrepreneur must have the intuition to leave the path she or he is following in order to go and look for the treasure.

To do all this you must be organized, rigorous and methodical, but you must also have a spirit of improvisation. The entrepreneur must have the intuition to leave the path she or he is following in order to go and look for the treasure, as this may not be on the main road. But you must never lose sight of that path, so that you can eventually return there and continue your journey.

But how does the entrepreneur do all this?

When launching a company, you need to know how to do a little bit of everything: that is why a startupper must not be too good at only one thing. Or rather, she or he must be ready to manage all the various processes that that phase involves. That is why the startupper is generally not a geek, but a dynamic person ready to 'get her or his hands dirty'.

A startupper must not be too good at only one thing.

I know, you are probably thinking of Mark Zuckerberg, who is one of the most famous startuppers in the world and who certainly is not (or was not) a guy like that, and is more typical of the nerd permanently glued to the computer. But he had the intelligence to surround himself with people who were different from him and who could make up for his shortcomings when it came to setting up Facebook.

I have always had this tendency to take care of everything, even pains in the neck. For example, when I was in high school, I was always the class representative, the school representative, the captain of the athletics team, the editor of the newspaper and the drummer in the school band. Then in the fifth year I realized that, if I wanted to pass my exams, maybe I should also study!

My ability to multitask was severely put to the test throughout at least the first year after the launch of *The Blonde Salad*. When the idea of starting a blog took shape during conversations via Skype with Chiara, I started to study html, to watch tutorials on the internet and to learn how to make the graphics of a site. It helped me that at that time I was in Chicago, a terribly cold city, and so I spent a lot of time in front of my computer, at home, in the warmth! Apart from work and sport, I didn't have much to do, so it was not difficult to find the time to build up a basic competence on the subject. At first it was very simple, because we used the very common Google platform, which was called Blogspot. We started from the standard Blogspot platform, from which we could access the html code, and then made the changes we wanted.

Of course, when the business grew, I left it to those who were better at the technical side than me. I understood that my skills could be better used in other areas, such as interpersonal relations and customer management. But even this is a process and not something that you can know from day one: only by working can you learn how to spend your time in a fruitful way. When you start, it is normal as the founder of the company to take care of everything. However, as you start to build the business you need to be able to understand where your skills and resources can best be invested, just as you must do with the staff you employ, without giving in to the urge to control everything. Otherwise it is impossible to grow, because we are all human and we all have limits, which are represented by our time, energies and abilities. Beyond a certain level, it is impossible to continue growing on your own. Before you get there, however, when you are not yet a structured business, it is inevitable that the founder will be forced to do most, if not all, of the work, without being able to delegate anything to anyone. This means dedicating practically all of your time to your project. And that is where passion comes in: only with passion will you bear the inevitable sacrifices. You have to be ready to put all your heart into it and more!

Beyond a certain level, it is impossible to continue growing on your own.

In the early years of *The Blonde Salad* I was totally dedicated to work. I had more or less stopped playing sports, giving up one of the things I love most, and I was fully focused on the project. At the beginning I was often the photographer, assistant and producer, as well as meeting the customers. Once back home, I would spend my evenings writing emails, while she would prepare the content for the blog… and the next morning we would start again.

Even afterwards there were times when it was necessary to stay in the office well beyond the limits of normal working hours (also because at that point, fortunately, we had moved from the living room at home to a real office). The release of the new platform in 2014 and the launch of the e-commerce site in 2016 required our constant and complete commitment and presence, although we could now count on a large team of collaborators. In the early stages of a new project, however, those moments really are the norm!

The same thing happened in the first three months of Foorban: Marco and Stefano slept so often on the office couch that they started to leave their toothbrushes and pyjamas there. It also happened later, for example, when we opened a small Foorban corner in the new Amazon premises in Porta Nuova, Milan. Also in this case, my associates and I found ourselves simultaneously being involved in the ordinary management of our business and the realization of our mini-canteen at Amazon, with the installation of the refrigerators, the heated cabinets and all the rest. Being a startupper can be a demanding job, even on a physical level!

(I can't get no) Satisfaction

I am of the opinion that you should not live to work, but at the same time I think that work can give enormous satisfaction and fill your life. This does not mean that, in the name of work, it is inevitable to have to sacrifice all of your free time, let alone your personal relationships: this is something that I have never wanted to do. But life is made up of many phases, and there will be times when you consciously choose to devote yourself more to work and at other times to other pursuits. The important thing is to find a balance, remembering that even if you cannot dedicate yourself totally to your work, professional satisfaction has a great impact on personal happiness. If I am not satisfied from a work point of view, I become a pain in my private life too... and those close to me can testify to that! The first phases of launching a new project are particularly exhausting, because at the beginning it can be difficult to evaluate the success of your idea. Numbers, in this case, may not be a reliable parameter. Sometimes, in fact, an economic return is not seen for years, because the launch of the company lasts for so long that it burns through funds over a long period of time, until it eventually reaches a volume of business that is large enough to repay all the hard work by generating a profit margin. Revenues, however, should come immediately in the sense that, when launching publicly, a positive response from the market should be immediate (depending, obviously, on the nature of the business).

My two partners and I founded Foorban at the beginning of January 2016, but the first five months of the year were dedicated to setting up the business, with the creation of the app, the installation and organization of the kitchen, and the hiring of staff. We structured the company with the idea that within five months at most we should be starting to invoice, because we had collected enough funding for 12 months. In other words, we knew that we could afford not to earn anything for a certain period of time, during which we would only have costs, but then, slowly, we would have to start making money. In reality, things went better than expected: as soon as we launched the service, we immediately started to receive orders, because thanks to word of mouth, to the fact that we had planned advertising campaigns on Facebook and Google, we had made ourselves known to potential customers through social networks... in short, we had created a buzz before take-off.

So, as soon as we activated the service, we started billing, and then we grew day by day.

Small steps

To do things, and to do them right, you need time. I am thinking, for example, of all that is needed to create a collection of shoes and accessories, a sector that I know well and that I have followed for years thanks to the Chiara Ferragni Collection.

The initial input starts with Chiara who, being the creative director of the line, gives a general outline and suggests an idea to the team of designers, of which some stylists are more specialized in trainers, others in shoes with heels and accessories. That initial outline serves as a basis for starting the creative process: the designers submit their drawings to Chiara, who selects, modifies and directs their work.

At this point, a proper operational meeting is held with the production manager, the manufacturer and the sales manager. The first might say, 'That shoe is beautiful, but we will never be able to produce it below a certain cost'; while the sales manager might say, 'Considering the trend last season, we'll never sell it above a certain price'. After this analysis, the collection is defined once and for all, and is produced in a variable number of samples, depending on the need. The samples are distributed to the sales offices responsible for the various geographical areas (Europe, Asia, America).

The spring/summer collection is presented in July of the preceding year. Buyers from all over the world examine the samples and order various pieces from the collection. Orders are collected until about mid-September, but even by the end of July the first orders are being passed onto the manufacturer who, depending on how things are going, might start production of some of the products. This is then carried on through September, October and November. In December, the manufacturer sends the ordered quantities to the stores around the world, so that from January, after the sales have finished, they can display and sell the spring/summer collection.

To paraphrase the famous proverb, a collection of shoes is not created in a day. But that is true of any project that is well done!

MASSIMILIANO BENEDETTI   Web Entrepreneur, Marketing Director of Yoox Group Until 2012 and Independent Board Member for the US Subsidiary of the YNAP Group

The traditional nine to five desk job no longer makes any sense in the post-digital revolution era. Even in the most traditional companies – and even more so in the most innovative ones – you cannot sit in your office and wait for business; you have to go and look for it!

That is why I always advise to keep your eyes wide open. After all, thanks to the internet, access to information is much more immediate than it once was, and therefore exploring new horizons and seeking new partnerships is much more within reach. If I find out about someone who is on the other side of the world, but who can help me expand my business, there is a good chance that with a few clicks, a Facebook contact, Twitter and an email, I will be able to hook up with them. And then, maybe with a Skype video call and a flight, I can triple my business… just because I hooked up to the right channel.

I remember that in August 2005, when we had just started with Yoox and had a very aggressive target for the United States, I had to decide whether to stay in the office to keep up with business as usual or leave for Nevada to meet the founders of the LinkShare service, seeing the possibility that the business could triple in a year's time. Obviously I chose the second option and it went well… but there are still many people who, in a similar situation, would have remained attached to their chair, yet I am convinced that, in a world in which all distances have been reduced, even the formal ones, it is essential to move to go and look for opportunities and new horizons. I have always told members of the teams I have worked with that if they spend all week at the office sitting at their desks, they are obviously doing something wrong.

The traditional nine to five desk job no longer makes any sense in the post-digital revolution era.

Precisely because of the dynamism that characterizes our time and the speed of change nowadays, planning projects in the traditional way no longer works. When I was a consultant, I always repeated this mantra: in a life free of risk, everything is at risk. I still firmly believe that. Even when everything is going well, if you sit down you run the risk that the world will change overnight and you will not be able to keep up with the change. I remember what happened with mobile technology – those who worked on the web and were unprepared when it exploded lost so many opportunities.

In a life free of risk, everything is at risk.

In order not to be overwhelmed by the changes, I think there are two strategies to follow. The first is to always keep the bar very high. Even if you are sure that you have done everything well, being higher up allows you to deal with any unexpected event better and with more autonomy. The second is to think laterally. If you have the ability to see not only the straight road in front of you like everyone else but also those that come in from the sides, it is easier to understand what countermeasures to take when the main road disappears. The key to everything is not to be unprepared when the change comes, but to try to be imaginative and creative right from the start (and this, I must say, the Italians are very good at).

Note

1   Thiel, P and Masters, B (2014) *Zero to One: Notes on start ups, or how to build the future*, Random House, New York.

CHAPTER FIVE

Together we will go far... and also faster

- *The importance of people in a company.*
- *Working with friends.*
- *The advantages (and disadvantages) of having one or more partners.*
- *Managing your staff.*
- *Strategies for choosing the most constructive partnerships for your business.*

All for one

A company is nothing in itself. A company is a group of people. For this reason, laying the foundations for a successful company means above all learning to invest in people. The premise, obvious but indispensable, is that you should not consider employees as numbers, but always treat them with the utmost respect. Apart from this, I am deeply convinced that a large part of the investment must be made in human capital, because it is absurd to think that you can build a company, and then grow and innovate, all by yourself. The syndrome of self-sufficiency characterizes a certain old-style entrepreneurial mentality, but alas it also affects many young entrepreneurs. In my opinion, however, it is a disaster, because climbing alone is impossible. Building synergistic and cohesive work teams is one of the crucial aspects to laying the foundations for a successful company, and it is even more important than having exceptional individuals in your team, because if they are not supported by a team that enables them to express their full potential, their qualities will be wasted. It would be like having Cristiano Ronaldo in a disorganized team, badly prepared in the field: if nobody passed him the ball, he would never be able to score and his hiring would have been just a terrible waste of money.

Climbing alone is impossible. I have always been convinced of this and it is reflected in the choice of the name of the company that Chiara and I founded in 2011. We called it TBS Crew because we liked the concept of a crew that undertakes a journey together and wants to continue going in the same direction.

When you leave the initial phase where you do everything on your own and decide to be helped by a few collaborators, it is crucial to surround yourself with people you know you can get along with. In a small business it is better to have pleasant people around you, and not only for the pleasure of working with them but also because the business will work better. On more than one occasion I have had the opportunity to verify that having a difficult person, regardless of his or her skills, in a small team creates complex situations and prevents that person – and those around him or her – from working at his or her best. Then, of course, the dynamics and needs of a team evolve as it grows: in a company with 50 employees, having a top dog is important, not just because they will almost certainly find someone to establish a positive relationship with. If there are 15 employees, however, it is better to dispense with the top dog if their character or attitude makes them unable to relate to their teammates.

To avoid being squeezed into a predefined mould, take care how you select the team you surround yourself with.

Being able to create a satisfying situation around yourself and not having to squeeze into a predefined mould is a concept that can also be applied to the team of collaborators you choose to surround yourself with. You have to be aware of what you are and surround yourself with people you get along with. I always refer to small and contingent realities, such as startups, because in a big company you cannot expect to all be friends and go to yoga together!

Friends, never... or maybe?

My personal experience is characterized by a strong mixture of friendship and business. At first it was a bit of a coincidence, dictated by the fact that my first important enterprise, *The Blonde Salad*, was born of a collaboration with my then girl-friend. After a few months, when the workload increased, we asked a few friends to come and help us out. At that time, we could not afford to hire employees, and in fact it would not have even made sense to work with professional photographers or graphic designers, given the still small size of our business. It was much better to do it with people it was pleasant to spend time with and it was easy to find the right synergy.

So, for example, my friend Chiara Magnaghi joined us, who was finishing her thesis in law and did not want to dedicate herself exclusively to that. She wanted an experience that would keep her busy for three or four hours a day while she completed her research. I needed help with administration and accounting, so she came on board too. In fact, over time, she became so passionate about our work that, after graduating, she decided to review her future plans and not start her internship in a law firm as she had planned. She stayed with us for six more months, during which time she realized that she liked the job very much. However, she also realized that she needed specific training in the field and so she enrolled in a master's degree in marketing and communication. After the master's, as she is an extremely brilliant person, she was hired by Saatchi & Saatchi, which is one of the most important advertising agencies in the world. She worked there for three years as an account and project manager before returning, again as a project manager, to *The Blonde Salad*.

It is true that I have also had bad experiences. In one case, after a very fruitful collaboration with a friend, the professional relationship started to deteriorate and then broke down completely. And the working break-up coincided with the end of the personal relationship. In other cases, friends came to work with me, then afterwards everyone went their own way, but without any bad blood... and we remained friends, even if we did not work together anymore.

It goes without saying that, in the choice of collaborators, the friendship factor has never prevailed over the evaluation of personal merits. I am absolutely convinced that it is not right to hire someone just because they are a friend, both from the point of view of justice and honesty, and for the good of the company. But if a friend is objectively good too, why not take them on board? For me, friends were a very important resource, particularly because my circle of friends was formed essentially during my university years and my first work experiences, so most of the time they were people with a similar background to mine who were in my field and whose skills I knew.

Of course, I have often had to find collaborators without drawing on my pool of personal acquaintances, therefore going through the classic channels of scouting, CV analysis, research and interviews, especially when my businesses started to become larger. In the startup phase, however, when your working life is almost completely superimposed on your private life to the point of being confused with it and you spend entire days (and even nights) together with your colleagues, then being surrounded by people you know, with whom you have a strong empathy, who you care about and trust, is important. Or at least it was for me. In the case of Foorban, for example, the fact that my partners were also my closest friends made the time spent together more pleasant and the initial sacrifices more bearable.

The risk is that from a personal point of view something will break sooner or later, because, if you consider that you are together so much for work, maybe in your free time you prefer to be with someone else, not because you care for each other any less, but because you really need a break.

Union makes strength

Another peculiarity of my experience as a startupper is that I have never launched a project on my own. I am an extremely sociable person and I draw strength from having a team to carry forward with me, to lead. I have always been like this and I have always had a tendency to take care of situations. My friends expect me to organize the trips or evenings because I have always done that. And I like to do it because otherwise I would not feel useful. Having someone else to take with me gives me the right amount of sense of responsibility. I think that if I had been alone when faced with some obstacles, I would have given up much more easily.

For this reason I am happy to have partners, because I like to have fellow travellers with whom to share the journey and the satisfactions. And having them becomes even more important when there are no satisfactions to share, only failures and disappointments, because you can deal with everything much better when you are together. Of course, you may have a person next to you who, in a difficult situation, pulls you down even further, but in general I think that sharing the challenges of launching and managing a project with someone else is a positive thing, especially if you have the intelligence to have someone by your side who has complementary skills to your own and can somehow compensate for your shortcomings.

Sharing challenges with someone else is a good thing, especially if you have someone by your side who has complementary skills to your own.

Among other things, being in a partnership means you can grow faster and build something in less time that is more complete than what you would have been able to do on your own. Besides, I like having to deal with inquisitive people – others' points of view are always very important to me. It has happened to me many times that discussing things with others has made me change my mind, even when I thought I was convinced of my point of view.

In the startup phase this is all the more crucial, because when you have to jump with all your heart into a project it is good when everyone is involved in the same way, knowing that they are not just working to bring home a salary, but equally to build something that is also part of them.

Here, too, however, it is a personal thing – not everyone loves having partners or is able to work with them. This applies both to the owner of a business, such as a clothing store, a restaurant, an e-commerce website, and to the creator of a super-technological startup: there are those who, rather than having partners, prefer to wait in order to be able to do everything themselves (even if this means having to renounce a few opportunities) and those who, on the contrary, give the best of themselves when part of a team.

There is no point in denying it: partnering up with someone can also have negative repercussions. You may have judged your partner wrongly, for the simple reason that it is almost impossible to know someone completely, or it may be that the person you are with changes over time. After all, people change all the time, depending on what happens to them in their lives. And those we are supposed to know may change when dealing with money.

In my opinion, however, the greatest risk when you have a partner is that, at some point along the way, the interests that previously were shared stop being so, and you are no longer looking in the same direction. Then some degree of friction is inevitable. Of course, there are many ways to get out of such situations, and instruments such as company statutes and shareholder agreements are there to regulate relations between partners, to prevent conflict situations or to help by safeguarding the interests of the company. When you start, it is natural to have a lot of momentum and think that everything will go well, but these steps should never be overlooked and it is essential to take advantage of the advice of professionals who can help those who are starting a project to have a very clear vision and provide solutions to solve all the problems that may arise in the evolution of a business. At the beginning, as in any kind of relationship, it is impossible to predict exactly what the project will become and how we ourselves will change during this process, so having clear agreements is of vital importance.

The greatest risk in having a partner is that, at some point, the interests that previously were shared stop being so, and you are no longer looking in the same direction.

Guiding others to do great things

Whether you founded a company alone or together with one or more partners, if things go well there comes a time when it is necessary to learn to delegate, and at that point the entrepreneur must devote at least half of his or her time to managing human resources. Again, this is a skill that is refined over time by means of trial and error. At the beginning it may happen that the wrong person is given too much responsibility, maybe overestimating someone or underestimating someone else... and only experience teaches us how to limit errors (knowing that it is very difficult, if not impossible, to get rid of them altogether). The guideline should be to bring together people that complement each other, to avoid conflict. A close-knit team cannot be made up of only strikers; neither can it be made up of only defenders. Again, knowing how to measure the various ingredients is essential.

A close-knit team cannot be made up of only strikers; neither can it be made up of only defenders.

Then, once chosen, the collaborators must be managed. In the past, the image of the successful businessperson almost always corresponded to an aggressive and authoritative figure, who had to constantly emphasize his or her own ego, while in the entrepreneurs of my generation a 'gentler' and more collaborative approach is more popular. It is the difference between being a boss, that is, the person who commands, and being a leader, that is, the person who leads his or her team and who becomes its point of reference.

I think that the choice between these two models depends very much on your own individual attitude. I, for example, could not be a boss even if I wanted to, because I am very empathetic. Precisely because of my personal nature, when the time comes that a collaborator who has made a mistake must be severely reprimanded, I would not be able to do it, and in any case, I would not be entirely credible. It is more natural for me to take the employee aside, make them understand what the mistake is and explain to them the reason for my disappointment and displeasure. It is a more humane process, which undoubtedly entails a greater expenditure of energy, but which almost always leads to a positive result. Despite this, I would not entirely demonize the boss attitude, because a bit of healthy realism suggests to me that sometimes, in certain situations and with certain people, it could be the most effective approach.

Another aspect that I feel is important in the creation of efficient and cohesive teams is to provide clear and precise information, so that everyone knows what their responsibilities are and the limits of their field of action. This is the only way to prevent conflict situations in which someone feels stepped on by a colleague. And this is also a way to motivate employees who feel they have defined roles, clearly know what is expected of them and what the objectives are that they must achieve. It is important that everyone is always informed of the general situation and at the same time that personal responsibilities are precisely defined. Bestowing responsibility is the best way to motivate, whereas pulling someone's chestnuts out of the fire is never a good idea. If you realize that a person is not able to do what they should be doing, you can take away their responsibilities, but taking on their duties and saying 'I'll do it for you' is no use to anyone.

Bestowing responsibility is the best way to motivate.

In order to motivate your team, it is very important that those at the top share information with everyone else. In the past, many managers used access to information as an element of power, without realizing that this negatively affects workflows and, consequently, the quality and speed of the work itself.

In addition, as I see it, you cannot share the company's objectives and results without also sharing the revenues: if it has gone well regardless of expectations, employees have every right to a bonus. I am convinced that in personal life money should not be a goal in itself, but simply a means of achieving other things.

In professional life, however, it is a reward. If an employee has worked and achieved results that are better than those set for them, it is only fair to give them an economic bonus. At the same time, if the work has been done correctly but the objectives have not been achieved, the employee should not be punished, because many variables can lead to failure. If, on the other hand, the failure to meet the targets is due to a lack of commitment on the part of the employee in question, it may be necessary to review their position, not least in order to set a good example to others. If, within a team of 10 people, nine work as they should and one does not, if no action is taken on the latter, all the others will be discouraged. The economic incentive is not just a prize but a way of recognizing the merits of an employee.

I realize that all this can seem quite obvious when you think of large companies and the manager who dishes out money that is not his or hers when it comes to deciding whether or not to grant a bonus to an employee (and even then, we know very well that you cannot take anything for granted!). But it is a much more delicate issue for small entrepreneurs, for whom such a decision can involve a significant personal sacrifice and therefore becomes a very important strategic choice.

Of course there are many other ways to boost the performance of the individual employee: there are startups where all of the company's profits are shared; others in which some employees, considered strategically important for the company, are paid through stock options, as was the case for example with Yoox (imagine having even only 0.1 per cent of the value at which Compagnie Financière Richemont bought it at – that is, 0.1 per cent of about 5 billion euros!).

Added to all this are the 'fun' incentives, such as corporate travel, team building events, sports tournaments, the weekly aperitif together…. These are activities that have nothing to do with the company's main activity but allow the team to get on better and become more and more productive.

Til death us do part (or almost)

When you set up a company, you should not only be concerned with your own employees but also with those of the companies you use to keep your business going. In this respect, the best thing is to aim for long-term relationships. When you want to do business together, you should make a serious commitment to your partner, which I compare in some ways to a wedding. You start with the idea that the business that you are laying the foundations for will not crash in 12 months' time but will be built over the medium to long term, so it makes no sense to think of exploiting your partner in the short term. Furthermore, if your partner is not a fool (and hopefully not, if you have decided to work with them!) he or she will be the first to want to set up a relationship of this kind, knowing that the real opportunity to make their work bear fruit and therefore to earn money is in the medium to long term.

That is what Chiara and I did with the Chiara Ferragni Collection footwear licensee, at the suggestion of our company's sales manager, Lorenzo Barindelli, who is a real point of reference for me.

We met when I told my mother that we wanted to create a brand of accessories and she, who has always worked in the field of clothing and had known Lorenzo for many years, suggested that I talk to him about it. Despite the age difference, we fell in love professionally, so much so that he became our partner. I learned a lot from him, because Lorenzo is so far ahead: his mind is much younger than half of my peers and his avant-garde mentality is combined with his vast experience. This is something I have always valued greatly and gained inspiration from, particularly because, at the time we started working together, I had such limited experience.

When you want to do business together, you make a commitment almost as serious as a marriage.

Thanks to Lorenzo's intuition, we decided to fully involve the producer of the Chiara Ferragni Collection in our project, as well as giving him some shares in our company. And the owner of the company in question, Pasquale Morgese, has fully repaid our trust over the years. From our first visit to the Mofra Shoes factory, he made us realize that he wanted to invest and launch himself into new projects and he believed in us so much that he enabled us to grow. For example, for the first season, he decided to produce many more shoes than had been ordered, because he was convinced that by the middle of the season the shops would have sold out and want to restock them. He took a great risk, because if his prediction had not turned out to be correct, he would have had a lot of shoes to dispose of and a huge economic loss. But his courage was rewarded: by the middle of the season we had sold out of not only those in the first order, but also all those in the restock.

Finding a partner who believes very much in your project is fundamental and, in my experience, it is the most important element to keep in mind when choosing them, without stopping at a superficial evaluation and perhaps only taking into account the other prestigious partnerships that they can already boast about. Pasquale made it clear that, for us, he would go to the moon and back. Shortly after starting our collaboration, in fact, he purchased another production facility just for the Chiara Ferragni Collection. And if that is not a sign of faith, then...

Building a company sometimes means forgoing short-term economic benefits and instead working towards what can be built in the long term.

Following a clear strategy in choosing the most constructive partnerships is really crucial. In the early stages of *The Blonde Salad*, for example, we often decided to work at zero budget but with high-profile brands that would help us build up our image. In other words, we decided to make sacrifices, aiming for a more important result but further away in time. At the time there were already many other companies that would have liked to collaborate with us, but we chose our collaborations in a far-sighted and wise way, working even without being paid for important names in the world of fashion, in order to build the positioning of our brand.

What *The Blonde Salad* is today, its international recognition and credibility, is the result of those very choices. After all, building a company sometimes means being able to forgo the economic benefits of a collaboration, because you have a clear idea of what can be built in the long term.

MATTEO SARZANA   General Manager Deliveroo Italy

Deliveroo is a global brand, but a hyperlocal business. This means that the brand, which is the same everywhere, is combined with a local business, which is particularly local because it is about food – perhaps the most locally connoted expression of all.

Even within the same national territory, in fact, as is the case in my country, Italy, eating habits can be profoundly different. This means having to combine a service that is the same all over the world with the need to adapt our strategy to completely different markets. We are therefore faced with a continuous dichotomy between the need to convey the essence of the brand and the need to vary it according to the habits within the context in which it operates… and this is something that can only be done if you know the local habits very well. Local also in terms of business relationships – in Italy, unlike in other countries, there are very few restaurant chains and therefore Deliveroo must create and manage local relationships on an individual basis. The fragmentation is huge and it is necessary to maintain a really good balance in order not to lose sight of the overall

It is necessary to maintain a really good balance in order not to lose sight of the overall picture – while still keeping a close eye on the local scene.

picture – while still keeping a close eye on the local scene, which is the one that keeps the business going.

A company like Deliveroo can use three levers: the price that is offered through our service; the selection, or the quantity and quality of restaurants with which we collaborate; and the service we offer. For the first two levers, anyone can act, because our competitors can copy everything from us. For the third lever it is very difficult to have an impact, because it represents the DNA of the company. That is why we try not to lose sight of the importance of providing an excellent service to our customers: the fixed rate for each delivery on orders that are forwarded through our app is a guarantee of quality. If something goes wrong in the management or delivery of the order, our operators try to solve the problem as quickly as possible, so as to leave the customer with the memory of a positive and satisfying experience. Of course, the concept of service is understood in its entirety – not only for customers but also for the partners and people who work for us.

CHAPTER SIX

Italians do it better?

- *Take on the global market aware of your uniqueness.*
- *The importance of social media in the global marketplace.*

It's a small world!

Whether you love it or hate it, globalization is a reality. And anyone who wants to do business must abide by the rules of the game. Of course, you may want to change them, but if you stick to them and interpret them correctly, it will be easier for you to succeed.

Today there are no longer any boundaries, thanks largely to the digital revolution in communication. And this applies not only to businesses directly linked to the internet, which by definition do not have those boundaries, but also to all the others. Before, for example, luxury brands priced the same product differently, depending on where it was sold. Now, however, consumers have cottoned onto this: first of all they can easily find out about it through a simple search on the internet, and, second, they can physically move from one country to another with an ease that was unimaginable until a few years ago.

Globalization, in short, has destroyed the so-called advantages of the nation: the barriers of entry dictated by geographical limits no longer exist and therefore a business must inevitably think globally from the start. Those who set up a business today must take into account everything that can be found on the other side of the world, because otherwise they will place themselves in competition with only a small number of other players right from the word go, when instead they should be well aware from the outset that the arena is now much larger. And it makes no sense to get bogged down in the risks of such a scenario: it makes much more sense, instead, to consider its opportunities. Of course, on a global level, there is more competition, and there are many more players who can steal a piece of the market from us... but we can do the same and steal a piece of the market on the other side of the world! It would be absurd to exclude so many opportunities right from the outset. Moreover, the competition is so fierce that often only the wide diffusion of a business can allow it to survive. Today there are many companies that have amazing turnovers but still do not have any profit margins, and they have to conquer half of the world before they can become truly profitable. This is the case with Uber, but also with a food delivery company as large as Deliveroo, which has such low profit margins that it has to be present in dozens of cities around the world to be able to optimize all economies of scale and be truly efficient.

Those who set up a business today must take into account everything that can be found on the other side of the world.

The fact that today there are no more boundaries also means that culture is slowly becoming homogenous. The negative impact of such a reality does not escape me, such as the loss of many local aspects, but I am also aware of the greater ease with which we can therefore communicate and understand each other. And this, from a business point of view, is without doubt an advantage. For example, the fact that the US chain Starbucks has exported the coffee culture all over the world means that those who want to launch a cool coffee brand that is superior in quality to Starbucks can now do so knowing that it will be easier to make the value of their product understood throughout the world. In short, if you manage to fit your own business into this global culture, if you think of it from the beginning as something that can be recognized and competitive on an international level, the opportunities for growth are endless.

Think globally

When launching a new project you have to always start with the idea that it could reach into every corner of the world, also because changing direction halfway through and adapting your idea to a global scenario is much more complex. Obviously, there are businesses that are localized, but in principle this argument is always valid, regardless of what you do: even a localized business par excellence, such as a bar in the centre of Milan, could become a chain, open more sales points in the city... and then, who knows, end up becoming a global franchise!

This philosophy has guided and still guides all my entrepreneurial choices. For example, with Foorban we are already thinking about what the next markets could be after Milan, and our global approach is drawing us not to other major Italian cities, such as Rome or Turin, but to major international financial centres, such as Frankfurt or Munich. It is more complicated, but there are certainly many more opportunities. What guides us in our choice are considerations of a cultural nature (consumers in financial cities are more accustomed to the idea of having their lunch brought to the office and eating it quickly, perhaps even in front of the computer), logistical (the speed of delivery is essential and in a large and chaotic city like Rome everything would be much more difficult) and practical (our typical customers are those who work in the business world and in other Italian cities the concentration of companies is not as high as in Milan or, indeed, Frankfurt or Munich).

That this has been our philosophy from the beginning is also clear from our choice of a non-Italian name. It is true, when it comes to cooking, that Italian cuisine has great prestige, but we wanted a more modern, more international interpretation, so that when we expanded to other countries and adapted our menus to the eating habits there, we could continue to be credible.

The same goes for *The Blonde Salad*: even in that case we chose an English name and we started to produce content in English right away. It may seem a triviality, but it is an important triviality, because from day one we imagined that people from all over the world would access our content. We did not limit ourselves to thinking that just one market would be our sphere of reference. Producing content in English has had a series of important repercussions, including of a technical nature, linked to indexing and visibility on search engines. It was not only a question of capturing individual readers and enabling them to read our content in a language they could understand but also of getting our site recognized in a different way to the whole internet structure: in fact, the domain is TheBlondeSalad.com and not TheBlondeSalad.it.

For the same reason we have not aimed for local editorial content because it would not have been of global interest. Instead we have gone for international content, very often US, because it has the greatest appeal worldwide.

Obviously, a global perspective must not lead to the specific features of local markets being overlooked. The case of the Chiara Ferragni Collection is interesting because it shows how a product designed for a global market can nevertheless be adapted to the different needs of national markets. For example, footwear for Asia is produced with a lower heel, as Asian women generally have smaller feet and prefer not to go beyond 6 cm heels. This means adapting the models – and it is not as easy as you might think: not only must the heel be lower, but the upper needs to be shorter too. So our product has been global and transversal since its conception and, for this very reason, adaptable to all the markets of the world.

A global perspective must not lead to the specific features of local markets being overlooked.

Different is beautiful

The fierce competition faced by businesses today can only be circumvented through differentiation, which is the main route to gaining a market share and asserting yourself. Marketing guru Jack Trout has summarized this principle in the famous formula *'differentiate or die'*.

When we created Foorban, Marco, Stefano and I kept it in mind, trying to imagine something completely different from what the Italian market offered and create a niche that did not exist. After having conceived of the initial idea – that is, trying to do something in the field of food delivery in Milan, which in our opinion still offered so many opportunities – we looked around. The players that already operated in this sector were all very large, very entrenched and, above all, had huge capital. So we couldn't even think of competing with them, mimicking them, in their own back yard: our resources, insufficient compared to theirs, would never permit us to do so. The only way we could compete was to try something different.

The fierce competition facing businesses today can only be circumvented through differentiation.

First, we identified the weak point of our competitors, which in our opinion was the delivery of the lunch. Because of their business model – customers consult the complete list of restaurants that deliver to their address, choose from the dishes offered by the restaurant they prefer, order and wait for the order to be delivered, all through their smartphones or computers – the choices for the customer are very complicated and delivery times become extended. At lunchtime, people, who are mostly workers on a lunchbreak from their office, are usually in a hurry and do not want to complicate their lives by having to choose from infinitely varied menus. In short, for a lunch it would be sufficient to be able to choose from a few simple and linear menus, offering healthy, light and good food. We understood that our product should reflect these aspects and stand out thanks to its speed and ease of use compared to other players in the market.

Of course, it was necessary to develop a completely different approach in terms of communication as well. Since the larger resources of the other players enabled them to choose an aggressive approach (pervasive advertising campaigns with public transport and building façades plastered with their billboards), we went in the opposite direction, with communication based only on word of mouth through social networks. Among other things, our competitors cannot communicate by focusing on the product, because they deliver the food prepared by so many different restaurants and, therefore, if the customer enjoys a good dish delivered from a certain restaurant, he or she will speak well – quite rightly – of the restaurant, but not necessarily of those who delivered it to them. We have done what other players cannot do: cook well and speed up the delivery as much as possible, creating an absolutely unique service in a market like Milan.

Uniqueness is the winning card, especially when you have few resources.

And there is already someone who has chosen to copy us and so is not following a path of uniqueness. But that is absolutely fine.

Just because there is already someone doing something, it does not mean someone else cannot do it too: the market, no matter how crowded, is big and there is space. You can also try to do something that others are already doing, but better than them. In principle, however, uniqueness is the winning card, especially when you have few resources.

The true Italian (but without a guitar in hand)

Precisely in light of the need to differentiate yourself from all the others, especially in a global scenario, 'Italianness' can be an important aspect. In my opinion, globalization is rewarding us: it has generated the need to find some seal of guarantee, and the Made in Italy merchandize mark is a value recognized everywhere. Unfortunately, however, I do not think that we are exploiting it enough. In some sectors, Italianness is truly synonymous with quality: in fashion, of course (and *The Blonde Salad* benefited from this at the beginning of its adventure, because being Italian made us more credible in the eyes of the world), food, obviously, but also in fields such as automotive and tech, in short, in everything that is design and product.

I believe, however, that we must not make the mistake of sitting back and relaxing thanks to this awareness of thinking, as unfortunately we have done and still do, that the mere fact of being Italian is enough, or that all you have to do is propose a stereotyped image of Italianness to the rest of the world. Our home market is very small, almost ridiculously small, and therefore it is important to communicate our value abroad, tell the world that the Made in Italy mark is modernity, research, innovation, design and quality of materials. And then we must work to make it clear that Italianness is not only about style, taste and savoir faire but also about professionality: something that we often lack in the eyes of the world.

Follow me

As I said, globalization has made competition very fierce and so being found by customers is not so easy. At the same time, however, the advent of social media has offered everyone an inexpensive tool to make a name for themselves with a potentially endless audience, and not only in terms of informing them about the launch of a new product but also in terms of entertaining them. In short, I think social media is an amazing tool. For the presence of a company on social media to be effective, however, it is necessary to understand its mechanisms and to know how to use them. This means a lot of things.

First of all, we must never lose sight of the fact that social media is precisely that, 'social media', that is, made up of people. Sometimes I offer my advice to companies that are taking their first steps on social media and they are surprised if, for example, the three photos of their bags they have uploaded are not liked by their followers. For me, however, it is not at all surprising, because I know that for content to be interesting, it must refer to someone's personal story. These media have in a sense globalized the concept of Big Brother, who was perhaps its forerunner: at the base of that mechanism there was the idea that an unknown person could become a means of communication. In this case, however, they became that means of communication through an already existing medium, television, whereas today it is digital technology that offers the individual that possibility to become a channel of communication.

Today digital technology offers the individual the possibility to become a channel of communication.

And it is precisely on the power of people's stories that this type of communication must focus, because people have decided that real stories are more interesting than invented ones. For this Instagram is the best tool. On Twitter you can mainly give

78

information and cultivate relationships with customers; on Facebook you can have a page that becomes representative of the world of the company and that certainly helps that company to be found, while Instagram is perfect for telling the story. And the consumer today expects the company to tell its story.

That social media is not all the same is a concept that those who create online communication must bear in mind. You have to have in mind what you want to tell your public, what you want to tell to all of your target audience. But then you have to communicate it in a different way depending on which of the social media you are using, because each of them is a place in itself and has its own specific characteristics. Applying the famous concept of 'glocalization' to this, you could say that the message is global, but the way it is communicated corresponds to the 'local' logic of each social media. To say the same thing on Instagram, Facebook and YouTube, you have to use different languages… and basically it is a bit like translating the same message into different languages.

If you are not able to tell a story and entertain your audience, I think it is better not to be on social media at all. When I see businesses that have 300 followers on Instagram, I think that they are only giving a negative image of themselves.

Put your face on it

And then, of course, you have to be able to relate to your customers, expect criticism and learn to react appropriately. In this case, in my opinion, the normal ethical rules that apply to discussions between people also apply here. If someone criticizes a product in a pretentious way, deliberately insulting it, there is no need to answer: there are criticisms that, as a brand, are not worth paying attention to (to put it bluntly, faced with a deliberate insult I would not answer even in a personal capacity). If, on the other hand, the criticism is well founded, perhaps because the customer has bought a product and is dissatisfied, it is advisable to respond publicly by offering to replace the defective product. In this case, social media gives you the opportunity to show everyone how well your customer service works. You must not be afraid of mistakes, much less of criticism: in my opinion you have to be more afraid of not being able to handle a mistake. At the same time, however, it is important to defend what you do and not bow to all kinds of criticism in the name of the logic that says the customer is always right: your business decisions must be owned.

You should not be afraid of mistakes; you should be afraid of not being able to handle a mistake.

I have been using social media to do business (and not only) for many years and I have understood that, both as a private individual and as a company, we need to try to understand who we should and should not listen to. The hatred that is unleashed on social media is the flipside of the coin with respect to the immense opportunities that it offers. At the beginning of the adventure with *The Blonde Salad*, I did not sleep at night. We were innovating, we were creating something new in the delicate sector that is fashion... and what is more, we were putting our faces on it. It is hard to imagine two people who could be more criticizable than us by those who wanted to do it! In the early days I tried to discuss and reason with the haters who attacked us with such aggressiveness. Then I realized that it was not worth wasting time and energy on something that serves no purpose. Not everyone will like me and I do not want to convince everyone: and it is fine like that. When you expose yourself, you need to be aware that you will run into hostility from someone. It is part of the game and you have to accept it.

This is just one of the many imperfections related to the world of social media and the problems and challenges that its use poses. But this does not diminish its power, usefulness or beauty; it is up to us to learn how to use it.

EMANUELA PRANDELLI Professor of Marketing at the SDA Bocconi School of Management and Director of the Masters in Fashion, Experience and Design Management (MAFED)

The positioning of a product or brand within the market of reference is one of the most important and delicate strategic decisions that a company has to make, since it is a fundamental driver of its competitive advantage.

Dealing with the competition rests on the ability to position yourself clearly and distinctively in the perceptions of the customers you intend to address as a priority, creating marked elements of preference in the mindset of the latter that are increasingly based not only on a product of superior quality but also on an impeccable service and an experiential component that is becoming more and more important in terms of guiding the choices of progressively sophisticated consumers. This implies, first and foremost, a surgical ability to segment the market – based on increasingly rich and articulated information that contributes to feeding the fascinating ecosystem of big data that companies today have access to for the first time in history – and an even more important ability to identify their target audience, which must then guide every decision and operational action, to create and consolidate a coherent image that can represent a fundamental asset for the company. This can mean occasionally forgoing short-term profit opportunities in order to not compromise one's integrity and to maintain distinctiveness in the long term in the eyes of the market segment one intends to target, undertaking with great awareness any brand extension strategies in order to avoid any form of cannibalization or in any case dilution of the original brand in the perception of key customers.

The positioning of a product or brand within the market is one of the most important and delicate strategic decisions.

In other words, without an accurate identification of one's target market at the start, there is a risk of being perceived as a schizophrenic further down the line, with the very tangible consequence of disorientating, or even antagonizing, demand and jeopardizing the very sustainability of the business in this way. And if this is true for any company in any sector, it is all the more relevant in the world of fashion and luxury, where image is crucial to defining the DNA of the brand and creating solid motivations for preference in a context where consumption is by definition symbolic and the value of the brand is indissolubly linked to the authenticity and exclusivity it is able to convey.

CHAPTER SEVEN

The no's (and yes's) that help you to grow

- *The importance of positioning and loyalty to yourself.*
- *Knowing how to say no – and sometimes yes – in order to build your own brand.*

Are you going to keep letting yourself be chosen or are you finally going to do the choosing?

That life, even professional life, is studded with continuous choices is a reality that we all experience. Founding some companies and having to manage them in the early stages of their lives has taught me that the choices you make at this stage are essential to the positioning of a company and for building and giving credibility to your brand. This means evaluating your partnerships well, studying your moves very carefully and also learning to say no.

I had such an experience in 2010, a few months after the birth of the blog. Chiara had been invited as a guest on a famous Italian television programme during Milan Fashion Week to comment on the fashion shows. We were then asked if she would be available to become a regular guest of the programme, as a commentator. The proposal was tempting: we knew that this would make her very popular and we imagined that we would also earn something from it, which was frankly unexpected at that time. We were just starting out, so it sounded almost crazy to refuse. Participation in a nationally important television programme would have given *The Blonde Salad* a visibility that it would have been impossible to achieve in any other way at that time.

Thinking about it, however, we realized that such a choice would be counterproductive for what we had in mind in the long run. What we wanted, in fact, was to become part of the fashion world, not that of show business, and we were sure that the European fashion environment, which tends to be snobbish and rather closed, would already have a hard time accepting a blogger like Chiara, and all the more so if her curriculum also included television. Of course, the no's are costly. That one and many others. And when you find yourself saying no, it is really hard. In retrospect, or from the outside, it always seems easy, but at the time we were afraid.

In this sense, I really admire those who have the courage to pursue their dreams to the end and say all the no's (including to immediate gains) that that entails. I think I did it, perhaps only in part, because I do not really know yet what 'the' dream of my life is. When I compare myself with artists, sportspeople, people who have identified that dream and have decided to pursue and grab it without worrying about immediate gains, I feel a great respect for them, also because resisting being dazzled, or being led astray by the first opportunity because you think it will be the last, is very difficult. But you have to be aware that, if you are open to welcoming them, there are always opportunities in life.

That is why I do not think that what happened to me with *The Blonde Salad* was 'the' opportunity of my life. I certainly had luck and foresight: a train passed by, I jumped on it and from there I started to build something, one brick at a time. But if we always hold onto the curiosity and open-mindedness necessary to understand how the world changes and where it is going, it is impossible not to see and seize one opportunity after another.

If we hold onto the curiosity and open-mindedness necessary to understand how the world changes and where it is going, it is impossible not to see and seize opportunities.

Of course, this awareness stems from experience. Going back to that no, I have to admit that hindsight makes it easier to say that we were right to renounce the visibility and money we would have gained. At the time, we were really afraid. We thought about it for two weeks, day and night. The fear also came from the fact that we were afraid to step on someone's toes in an environment that we knew nothing about and had no idea about its *modus operandi*.

In reality, however, deep within ourselves, we knew it was the right decision: we did not feel ready to do something like that and we knew it would not take us where we wanted to go. It was the passion and sensitivity towards the world of fashion that guided us and made us understand what the way forward was.

Anyone who starts their project in any field should imagine and almost hope that among the thousands of opportunities that present themselves, such situations will occur, first of all because it is better to have many opportunities to choose from than to have to resign yourself to heading down a path that has already been walked, and second, because, despite all the effort involved, these are the very moments that make you focus on who you are and who you want to become.

Become desirable

The world of fashion and in particular the world of luxury is the one I know best and from which I have learned many things, especially with regards to knowing how to say no. This is a sector that has completely different dynamics to all other industries: it is the only one in the world where the less you sell the cooler you are. To keep the value of a brand high in the world of luxury, it is necessary to preserve it, to maintain it as a point of reference for a specific group of people, out of the reach of the masses.

Companies in the luxury sector – which at the end of the day need to make money, just like everyone else – use cosmetics as their true entry-level products. However, they do not deal directly with cosmetics, but rather entrust their production to third-party companies, which then distribute the products through other channels, not in the brand's flagship stores, and publicize them in a different way. By distancing itself as much as possible from the communication and distribution of its cosmetics, the company keeps the brand clean but at the same time makes money. For the consumer, however, buying a cream, lipstick or perfume is a way to enter the world of luxury without spending the impossible sums required for clothing or accessories. After all, these latter are not purchased for their comfort, utility or efficiency, but because they allow the buyer to enter a world of values and recognizability that they want to belong to. And for this to happen, access to this world must be restricted to a limited number of people. That is why luxury brands do not make unlimited quantities of their most affordable entry-level products available, such as smartphone covers. If everyone could have those covers, their appeal would diminish and, consequently, so would that of the more expensive products of the same brand.

The Chiara Ferragni Collection falls within these dynamics and we came up against those very dynamics at the beginning.

After selling many glittery flat shoes with the wink symbol, which were the most iconic and recognizable product in our first collection, we saw interest in them decline. The reason was that too many people had bought them and they were no longer distinctive: owning them no longer conveyed a sense of uniqueness. At our expense we learned a classic mechanism of the luxury market (and not only!): to keep the desire alive you have to be able to deny yourself.

To keep the desire alive, you have to be able to deny yourself.

There are many ways in which fashion brands implement this strategy and try to create desirability for their products: from a careful choice of prices based on the target audience you want to reach, to not making them available to all the people who want them.

Obviously, these dynamics do not apply to all sectors, even if the concept of desirability is a cornerstone on which the sale of any product or service is based. That is why, before launching into a market that you know little about or in which you have never operated, it is so important to study in depth its mechanisms and *modus operandi*, which today more than ever can change very quickly and which often also have counter-intuitive features. Continuing to do what has always been done and how it has always been done, or launching into an enterprise guided only by a romantic idea or by notions that are a legacy from other generations, without anchoring all this to a very concrete and realistic analysis of the landscape in which you move, could be the fastest way to burn your passion (and your investment) in the fire of harsh reality.

An overwhelming supremacy

At this moment in time, the New York streetwear brand Supreme is more successful than anyone else at creating desirability, having become a cult object like few others have managed. Born as a skater's shop, Supreme has made itself known in recent years through a widespread marketing strategy based essentially on its omnipresence on Instagram. What makes Supreme so cool is that it is very difficult to find its products anywhere. This is because they produce only a few of them and they are only sold online and in the brand's 11 official stores. Unlike normal clothing brands, Supreme is not subject to seasons, but every fortnight it launches capsule collections that are invariably sold out within a few minutes of being put on sale. The prices are not high, in line with the fact that it is a streetwear brand, but the scarce availability of the original articles feeds the mechanism of resale, and so there are those who are willing to pay for these items at even 10 or 20 times their original price. Because if you can turn your products into cult objects, collectibles, there is no limit to the price they can attract.

Supreme is currently one of the most significant case studies in the world, precisely because it has managed to create incredible power around its brand. In light of this, it is clear why a noble luxury company such as Louis Vuitton has entered into a partnership with Supreme. And it is really incredible that a fashion house with the history and fame of Louis Vuitton has chosen to combine its brand with that of a streetwear company to increase its own coolness. This deal is considered one of the best management successes of recent years – obviously by Vuitton and not by Supreme, which was already a success in itself – because it managed to create desirability around a historic brand like LV, making even the younger target consumers and the newly rich around the world want to buy products with a logo that until a few years ago was associated with a classic elegance. The fact that a structured and age-old company like Louis Vuitton, with such an important legacy, has had the courage to do such a thing, is definitely to be appreciated.

That the brand should be perceived as particularly cool by the market is especially important for fashion companies, particularly luxury companies, because when you pay for the value of the brand rather than of the object itself, the former must be seen as being very special. This mechanism, however, is not only valid for those who make clothing or accessories, it can also be applied in other contexts. Whether you want to launch a venue or a hotel, or offer a service, it does not matter: keeping these dynamics in mind when deciding whether to apply them or not is very important and can help everyone. Obviously, anyone who invents something that was not there before and is needed by everyone would not have to create this desirability, as it would come naturally. However, given that it is increasingly difficult to do such a thing, and that practically everything that is invented is simply an improvement or a reinterpretation of something that already exists, thinking about adopting these strategies is certainly a possibility.

If you go down this road, you need to be all the more patient and not expect to see initial results in just a short space of time. Desirability cannot be created overnight. It means being able to plant a mental seed in people's minds, so that for a thousand reasons they come to want that very thing: either because they saw an influencer wear it; or because they found out that there was an exclusive event that was difficult to gain access to; or because they were not able to grab hold of the product as there were too few of them, or it cost a lot and therefore only a few people could have it; or because a partnership with a very cool brand has been set up and therefore in the mind of the consumer the two brands have become linked.

Desirability cannot be created overnight.

But it takes a long time to do all this... unless you have really large resources at your disposal before you launch the product, and even then, it will always be a gamble. Because in the marketplace, as in life, nothing is certain.

The brand's prestige

The idea of making one's own brand a synonym for desirability and exclusivity is spreading through to many other sectors, from the automotive world to technology. It is the path that a social network such as aSmallWorld has also taken, which focuses on travel and lifestyle and is characterized by an exclusive access system based on the invitation of an existing member and subject to the approval of certain users. However, after some initial success, aSmallWorld has experienced a big decline, especially since the introduction of an annual membership fee in 2013. This made membership of the community much less cool, because you just had to pay to be a part of it.

We kept this mechanism in mind during the launch of Foorban. From the very first moment we understood that we would have to aim our food delivery service at a fairly high target audience, because our analyses clearly showed us that we would never be able to sell our dishes below a certain price, but to grow we needed to build a loyal clientele who would be willing to spend those amounts at least 15 times a month. We understood that to reach that target audience it was vital to generate word of mouth by getting those professionals who would be the best witnesses to the quality of our products to try our dishes. To create desirability with tools such as word of mouth and referral, as I said, takes more time, but the result was what we expected.

The products in the e-commerce section of *The Blonde Salad* answer to the same philosophy, because most of them are clothes and accessories that make up small capsule collections. For example, from time to time, Superga brand trainers are proposed, which are the result of a collaboration between the creatives at TBS and those of the company in question, and they are always a limited edition. The release is accompanied by an editorial on the website and posts on various social channels. The same with the bodies made by Yamamay: in this case three designs are sold exclusively on *The Blonde Salad* and three others in the brand's stores. The choice we made was to work on exclusive products that were only found on the website, just to create uniqueness and desirability.

The retail apocalypse

This system is already very widespread, and I think it will become even more so, partly as a response to the retail crisis generated by the spread of e-commerce and in general to the big changes that have affected the fashion world in recent years. Physical stores are no longer the only sales channel available, as there are myriad websites – from the company's own website to the large online fashion stores – that sell the same products.

Companies with a brand of enormous value, such as the aforementioned Louis Vuitton, but also Chanel, Gucci, Prada, to name but a few, can take advantage of this and make their stores real 'embassies': when the customer enters Chanel, they must feel like they are in the country of Chanel. From this point of view, the shop becomes a marketing weapon: whether the purchase is made there or a few hours later at home, online, is irrelevant at that point. That is why in the near future these big luxury companies will rationalize their stores, closing many and keeping only the so-called flagship stores, where you enter just to live an experience, to discover something new, to fall in love with the world of that brand. That total integration of online and offline is the future of the fashion world from the point of view of distribution is an incontrovertible fact. However, the mass market is different, because low-cost products, such as those of Zara, imply a much more impulsive purchase, so the more shops the customer finds around them, in the streets of their city, the more likely they are to buy.

Yet, as consumers, we know very well how much e-commerce has managed in just a few years to radically transform our habits, so much so that now any purchase – from books to cosmetics, from electronics to food – even when made in a physical store, is often preceded by an online search to compare prices, study the characteristics and read the reviews of a product. And the opposite is also true: maybe first you go to the store to see the item for yourself and then you go online to hunt for the most advantageous offer. Therefore anyone who wants to sell anything can, and indeed has to, think very freely about how to integrate the offer to and the reception of the customer between the point of sale and the site of e-commerce while taking into account all of this.

Returning to luxury fashion brands, and putting aside the discourse of the flagship stores, I imagine that in the future there will be only a few multi-brand stores in the world, but they will have a very recognizable style. And, just like *The Blonde Salad* online shop with its capsule collections, they will only sell products that the brands they distribute produce ad hoc for them. Otherwise, what would be the point of going shopping in such a shop if you could do it on the website of the brand in question, and have much more choice and, in some cases, lower prices?

What awaits us at the end of the catwalk

This theme is deeply linked to another big transformation in the fashion system that originates from communication. Previously everything was very schematic: a fashion show was organized in September in which only journalists and buyers took part, and, after seeing the collection, the latter placed their orders. The items presented at the fashion shows were produced and sent to the shops in January of the following year. In the meantime, journalists wrote the articles, interviewed the designer about the collection and prepared the editorials. Then between December and January those articles were sent to press, stimulating the curiosity of possible buyers who could then begin to buy, finding in the shops what had been shown on the catwalk months previously.

Now this system has changed: in addition to the journalists, there are also fashion bloggers and celebrities at fashion shows who photograph the models and post them immediately on social media. Potential buyers can see in real time items that have not – and indeed could not have – yet been produced because, especially in the case of high fashion, the creation time is quite long. It is also essential to receive feedback from buyers in order to start producing and therefore avoid waste. But today the time between when the garments parade on the catwalk and when the public is aware of them has zeroed out: consumers no longer want to wait three months to get what they have seen in preview thanks to bloggers.

The companies have responded in various ways. There are those who have implemented the '*see now, buy now*' strategy, offering the possibility of purchasing at least some of the garments and accessories just a few hours after they have been presented at the show, either online or in single-brand boutiques; there are those who have reduced delivery times to one or two months; and there are those who produce everything in advance, taking the associated risks, so that customers can make their purchases straight away. In each case, it works against the big buyers: inviting them to the fashion show, but then undermining them by starting to sell those same items the very same day.

Obviously fast fashion also has a hand in this phenomenon, because the companies in this sector have a two-week production chain and so, after having seen a model at a fashion show, they can copy it, reproduce it and sell it in a very short time, at a speed nobody can compete with. Of course, the quality is not the same, but today the buyer often gives more value to the style, to the coolness of an item of clothing, than to the quality of the materials or the care with which it has been produced.

These are very fast and very profound transformations that in just a few years have begun demolishing consolidated systems, with many interests at stake. As with everything related to the tumultuous times we are living in, it is difficult to predict what will happen and when. I venture the hypothesis that in the future fashion shows will no longer be concentrated in a particular period, but each brand will host one when and where it wants, because they will become simple moments of communication.

Embracing change

This reflection on the speed of change characterizing our time gives me the opportunity to illustrate another rather important concept. If it is true that the no's are fundamental and help you to position yourself, it is also true that you must also have the courage to say yes when necessary. For example, this may mean knowing how to recreate yourself by continually exploiting the tools available.

When we started with *The Blonde Salad*, Instagram did not exist. The app was launched in 2010 and since then this social network has seen an unstoppable growth, exceeding 800 million active users per month worldwide by the end of 2017. Among other things, the birth and growth of Instagram made many people around the world understand what we had already guessed when we created the blog: when it comes to fashion, users want content of a certain type, not necessarily produced by professionals, but rather by normal people who showcase their look. When this happened, we realized that we could not ignore it and continue to offer that type of content on our website. We decided to move it all onto Instagram and produce something completely different for *The Blonde Salad*, using ad hoc resources.

You need to know how to recreate yourself by continuously exploiting the tools available.

The photos posted by an influencer on Instagram are not the same as those of someone with a private profile since, while it is true that in some cases they are created spontaneously, in others they are the result of precise work, just like the photo-shoots of a glossy magazine.

With that yes to change, a completely new opportunity opened up for us, an opportunity that until then we had not even considered, namely that of creating an online magazine. Obviously, even when you do something like that, it is essential not to change your DNA and so, when *The Blonde Salad* became a magazine, it nevertheless remained very attached to the image and life of Chiara Ferragni. If, for example, she was dressed in pink, the magazine would show you all the most beautiful themed looks of the week. The aim was to always remain consistent with our history and character, while exploiting the tools and technological innovations that presented themselves to us.

Every change in strategy involves a yes, to be said out loud, with total conviction, even though we know that it is always a gamble that requires a good dose of instinct, but also the willingness to get involved and to take risks on channels and with tools that, because of their novelty, are untested and do not offer guarantees. And, even when using more traditional instruments, you have to bear in mind that changing strategy midway may mean having to use resources that you had not planned to have to use.

For example, in the run-up to the launch of Foorban, we had not even thought of creating a website from which to order. There would only be the app for ordering. But after three months of being on the market, we realized that very often professionals – who are our target audience – needed to have lunch ordered by their secretaries and that the latter preferred, for many reasons – personal, or even just for convenience – to place the order through the website rather than from their smartphone.

This has involved a huge unforeseen investment, with the development of a proper website to which you have to subscribe and which is synchronized with the database of the app… something not so simple, but absolutely necessary.

CHAPTER EIGHT

Tell a story and spill the beans

- *Use social media to raise awareness about your business.*
- *The importance of personal branding.*

To be present or not to be present?

'If you're not on social media today, you don't exist!'

This sentence is so banal and is repeated so often that when I hear it, it has the same effect as when I hear: 'Mid seasons no longer exist'.

Joking aside, it is obvious that, like all clichés, it also contains an undeniable truth. And in fact, as I said, I too am convinced that social networks are an extraordinarily effective and much cheaper tool than traditional ones to make yourself known to a potentially infinite audience. However, like all clichés, it is also a trivialization of a much more complex concept and therefore risks flattening a reality that is full of light as well as shadows, creating false illusions and perhaps even generating frustration in those who think that social networks are a marketing channel that is quick and easy to manage and then find themselves dealing with results that do not meet their expectations. Again, things are not as simple as they seem and, before entering the magical world of social media, you should understand the mechanisms and the rules.

The first myth to be debunked is that social networks are an unavoidable tool for the growth of every type of business. Because, while it may be true that they are fundamental when the product or service we want to sell is aimed at what in corporate language is called the consumer, when the target audience is other companies, so the product or service is the business itself, and the usefulness of social media is almost non-existent. In this case it is much better to use traditional tools to make yourself known, ranging from trade fairs (and yes, I know that this expression makes you think of a dusty reality and one that is definitely not *smart* and innovative, but today fairs are often crazy events and true conventions) to direct mail and LinkedIn, which is a social media, but with a very specific focus on companies and which, thanks to newsletters and marketing campaigns via email, can really

The first myth to be debunked is that social networks are an unavoidable tool for the growth of every type of business.

be a valuable tool in making yourself known. In this case, being on Facebook, Instagram or Twitter is completely useless.

Things are very different for those who have to promote their business to end consumers: in their case, social networks help to reach a very high number of potential customers with lower investments than traditional tools. These investments, however, must be well thought out and not seen only in terms of buying advertising. A lot of people still make that mistake and do not think about how important it is to create effective content. Buying advertising space in a newspaper costs more and reaches fewer people than a post on a social network, but those who decide to buy it know perfectly well that they have to ensure the quality of the content that will be published and the photo that might accompany it. Why is this not also just as normal when it comes to social media?

If we want to be effective, if we really want to reach people, we must strive to create content that matches what we intend to tell our followers in order to draw them in. If we create bad content it will be much more difficult to be heard. Those who use social media at a professional level cannot afford to have anything less than a very high standard of quality at all times. Having started my career with *The Blonde Salad*, which is a media company, all this has always been very clear to me. Of course, in our case, the content and entertainment of our audience was our core business and therefore the most important aspect of our work, not just a promotional tool. But I have not forgotten the lesson I learned then about the importance of creating effective content. In fact, with Foorban, I and my partners agreed from the beginning that social media communication should be a crucial part of our project and that is why we devote a lot of time and resources to it. We understood how important it was to present our potential customers with aesthetically pleasing photos, able to communicate the genuineness and goodness of the product even to those who, being on the other side of the screen, cannot, alas, smell its aroma. That is why from the start we collaborated with talented photographers and professional food designers. It is true that photos of food, along with those of kittens, are usually the ones that get the most likes on social media, but that does not stop us insisting that those of our dishes are also beautiful!

Not lost in translation

All of this today is – or should be – clear to all companies, regardless of their size. In fact, there are large companies that, thanks to greater investment opportunities, hire proper editorial directors to oversee the creation of all the content they need. It is not uncommon for large companies, especially in the world of fashion and lifestyle, to hire people who can guarantee editorial direction in brand communication. For example, it is quite possible that a men's clothing brand will hire the former editor of a magazine with the same target audience to manage the creation of content that will go on various social channels, newsletters and the website, which can no longer be a simple lookbook, but must present real editorial content

A unified vision is necessary because, as I said, having different communication channels means having to master different communication dynamics. It is a re-proposal of the famous principle *think global, act local*, although in this case it applies not to different geographical areas but to the different channels of communication. The editor in chief should transmit to his or her team a unified vision, which is then interpreted in different ways depending on the channel used, as if it were a translation into different languages of the same message. Naturally, for anyone who sells something, the ultimate goal is always to sell, but, given different tools, you can develop different tactics. It is obvious that I cannot put the same content on YouTube, Twitter and Instagram! If, for example, I sell bananas, for YouTube I would have to create a captivating video, complete with tutorials, on how to prepare a smoothie. For Instagram I should have a nice photo, because aesthetics and photography are the focal point of this social media. On Twitter, instead, I could post the link to an article that explains how the potassium intake of bananas has great benefits for health…. In short, the point is to be able to translate into the language of each channel the message I want to convey, that is, that eating bananas is good for you.

In some cases numbers do not count

Another very common mistake is to believe that numbers are everything. The point, instead, is not (only) to win over a large number of fans or followers but above all to engage, that is, to involve your audience and build strong links between them and your brand. Building your own online community is essential, as is keeping it active and involved. If you can do this, you will have at your disposal not only an army of potential customers but also real brand ambassadors who love your product and will talk about it on their social channels with the same zeal and passion they might have for a cause that is particularly dear to them. I am convinced that every person on his or her social channels is an influencer, regardless of how many followers they have. And social networks, which give us the opportunity to involve people, to network, taking advantage of the power of each to influence others, are in this sense a very powerful weapon. I always say that the real strength of startups – and also of larger companies of course – lies in people, and I believe that this logic can and should also be transferred into the world of social networks.

I am convinced that every person on his or her social channels is an influencer, regardless of how many followers they have.

Use what you have

A consolidated company has the possibility and resources to manage the various social channels and – hopefully – the awareness that each channel has its own language and rules, and that therefore it makes no sense to have several identical social profiles, all offering the same content. But we know very well that, when a project is in its initial stages, resources are scarce and therefore it is impossible to imagine hiring specialized people who can deal with these aspects of communication with all the care that an already solid company can reserve for it. In other words, it is clear that when you launch a startup, you cannot count on having a team of social media managers! However, this does not mean you have to give up using them: everyone involved in the project can try to follow its official social media profiles, just like they follow their own personal profiles. However, it may make sense to assign each member of the team a task, so as to achieve that level of specialization I mentioned earlier, trying to identify the person who has more aptitude in using YouTube, the one who knows Instagram better.... Of course, a startup does not necessarily have to use all these channels; it can instead focus very well on just one or two and exclude the others, depending on the type of service or product it offers, by identifying the community of reference that would be more interesting.

In general today Instagram and Facebook are the most used social media, so at the start the choice may be one of the two if you do not have the resources to follow both. Of course, the choice also depends on what the business is offering. If you do not have products that are beautiful to look at, interesting from an aesthetic point of view, it is pointless being on Instagram, which was created precisely for sharing images. If you sell a very technical product whose appearance is not particularly appealing, for example, it certainly makes more sense to be on Facebook, where you can give other types of information. If you are lucky enough to have someone on the team who can create and edit YouTube content, it is a good idea to take advantage of it... but I imagine that does not happen often because YouTube is a much more complex tool and the work needed to create quality content is greater and much more technical. As for LinkedIn, because of its business nature, it occupies a separate place from other social networks: Foorban is present and active on it, and our LinkedIn page will keep you informed about our activities, collaborations, job offers.... But these are all things that do not necessarily have to be part of the first phase of a business as they can be postponed to a later stage.

Great transparency... and a hint of cynicism!

For those who know how to use them properly, social networks can offer very concrete ways to create extraordinarily successful business realities. The web is full of bright examples, but a story that I find very inspiring is that of Cristina Fogazzi, a beautician from Brescia who owns a beauty clinic in Milan. A few years ago she started a blog in which she discussed themes related to the world of aesthetics with honesty and irony to encourage women to take care of themselves, but at the same time making them laugh. Her posts were accompanied by funny cartoons in which her alter ego – the Cynical Beautician – did not hold back on uncomfortable truths on topics that give many women sleepless nights, such as cellulite, pimples and wrinkles, with professionalism and a wealth of scientifically founded information, but also with an irresistible sense of humour. This new formula had an explosive success, which was consolidated by Fogazzi's skilful use of social media. The winning key to this project was, on the one hand, the originality of her approach that made her stand out from all the other operators in the sector, and, on the other, the very careful use of social media that allowed her to develop extraordinary engagement and a community of faithful followers who have great confidence in her and her advice and also in her products. In response to requests by her followers, Cristina Fogazzi also created a line of products that she reveals through social networks and sells on a dedicated e-commerce platform. Last year the cosmetics line of the Cynical Beautician managed to triple its revenues, going from 150,000 to 450,000 euros a month. What started as a nickname has become a successful brand, a solid company characterized by a business model that seamlessly intertwines online and offline commercial dynamics.

Another aspect to admire (and imitate) is the transparency of her social interactions with her followers, which earned her their trust and even their understanding when she made some inevitable mistakes. For example, when the e-commerce website had technical problems that led to temporary service interruptions and delays in the delivery of products, she admitted this with great sincerity, explaining both the difficulties and the countermeasures put in place to resolve them, and always with the irony that is her hallmark. Her community sympathized with her and rooted for the whole team, supporting them in the most critical moments. There is really something to learn from those who (also) know how to handle their mistakes so well, never losing confidence in themselves and their abilities while nevertheless showing great humanity and sincerity. It is not always possible to avoid negative events, but to have the quick-wittedness to handle them in this way, without denying them and apologizing if necessary, is a really good thing.

A company should always be transparent with its customers, whatever the channel used to communicate with them, but even more so on social media, which offers the opportunity to communicate directly and without intermediaries. However, it is of course naive to think that a company can show everything, because not everything is communicable to the outside world. So, for example, while it is true that we need to be transparent with our customers, it is also true that we need to protect ourselves from the competition and possible imitators. If my company, say, produces bags, I will certainly not show the models of the next collection before they are ready and distributed, because I cannot leave them to the mercy of all.

A company should always be transparent with its customers, whatever the channel used to communicate with them, but even more so on social media.

Striking, or rather epic, failures

Another thing that should never be forgotten is that the power of social media can also be negative. When you use social media, especially in business, you can never be too careful, because an error that is not immediately recognized as such can turn into an avalanche with unpredictable consequences. These are the so-called epic fails: they are very insidious and can make a brand unforgettable – in the negative sense, of course – in a matter of minutes, destroying the work of years in one fell swoop. A striking example was the social media campaign launched in China by Dolce & Gabbana in November 2018, on the eve of a fashion show scheduled in Shanghai: the concept behind the videos released through the brand's social media channels should have been the brand's love of the great Asian country. In practice, however, the videos were perceived as offensive by Chinese users, who considered the use of a series of cultural stereotypes about their country, their eating habits, even their precepts about beauty, to be inappropriate. The Milanese fashion house was forced to remove the incriminating videos after heated debates broke out on social media. As if that were not enough, however, after a few hours an Instagram account close to the fashion world published a series of private messages from the personal account of designer Stefano Gabbana, in which he gave vent to what had happened through rather unpleasant insults about the Chinese people. Although Gabbana later claimed that his profile had been hacked and that those messages had not come from his account, the damage was enormous: the main Chinese e-commerce sites stopped selling D&G products and Chinese users showed their disappointment with the brand by inviting their fellow users to boycott it.

While it may be true that social storms die down as quickly as they blow up and do not automatically mark the decline of a company (especially if it is large and important), but that at worst create a setback, it is also true that from the above case, and from many similar ones that have occurred in recent years, we can draw an important lesson: learning to use social media with care is crucial for anyone, and for a company even more so. We cannot share with impunity what pops into our heads, in terms of education first and foremost, but also because the consequences of our actions can be very serious. Social networks are a neutral zone and there is no distinction between the virtual world and 'real life'. In fact, expressing yourself unrestrainedly on social networks can be even more dangerous, because our words have a huge, virtually borderless sounding board. Precisely because many businesses today have a global dimension, it is unthinkable that anyone still believes they can use certain cultural stereotypes. What is acceptable, even funny, in one culture, could be very offensive elsewhere... and it would be good if everyone, but especially those who are responsible for a company and its many workers, always remembered this. It is pure arrogance to expect everyone to share our way of seeing things... or to laugh at our jokes.

Learning to use social media with care is crucial.

The only person you are destined to become is the person you decide to be

Social media is also phenomenal when it comes to personal branding, which is an expression that indicates the set of strategies put in place to promote yourself, your skills and experiences, your career, as if you were, in fact, a brand. And it is something that can be really useful to everyone to ensure that a customer, an employer or a partner chooses us. It is essential when you want to change jobs, when you are looking for new opportunities, when you are looking for a partner or a lender for your own project. The final objective of any personal branding operation, in fact, is to be able to communicate a credible and recognizable image of yourself, positioning yourself as if you were a company or a product… and it is not difficult to understand how crucial this is, especially in a labour market like the current one, where it is the norm to reinvent yourself time and again during your professional lifetime.

I have been building my own brand for a few years now. I have to admit that at the time I was not clear why, but my instinct told me that it was something that could help me in the future in order to develop any kind of project I had in mind, but also any kind of cause that was important to me and that I wanted to share with my community. Now that a few years have passed, I recognize that it has been and continues to be very important, mainly as a support to my serial startupper activity. I am convinced that for a serial startupper the time dedicated to personal branding is well spent, because it helps you to create a community of people who know you and trust you, giving you the certainty that, whatever professional project you decide to launch into next, they will still give you their trust. For those of us who do this work it is very important to show customers, investors, partners of our companies, that we are a dynamic person, who never stops growing and evolving. And of course it is extra work, because it cannot be left to chance or improvisation… but the rewards, in the long run, are very many.

In this regard, I have to say that I have found another advantage: precisely because I often work on new projects, my community is basically my first target audience to see whether an idea can really work. The members of my community are often the first I introduce it to, who I ask my questions of, trying to involve them in the process that helps me to understand if a new project is valid or not. And they are always the first to be involved in the launch if that idea comes to fruition.

If I had to indicate what you should base your personal branding on, I would undoubtedly stress once again the importance of authenticity and transparency: being yourself is the best way to build a credible personal brand. I think this is essential because social media in general is quite transparent and it is not easy to be credible in communication if you do not communicate something you really believe in. True to this principle, I have always tried to maintain the right mix of elements that make up my public image, which obviously corresponds to what I really am. On my social channels – especially Instagram, which is my favourite – I present the glamorous side of my business, made up of participation in events, fashion shows and everything else as well as the business side (which takes up much of my working day), that is, the hard work involved in the launch of a startup or, like being on the board of Foorban, the challenges of managing an innovative food company, without ever forgetting my great passions for motorcycles, travel, sports and music, which are by no means less important than everything else and which recharge my energy, as does my wonderful marriage to my wife Gabrielle.

Being yourself is the best way to build a credible personal brand.

Are you going to keep being influenced, or are you finally going to influence?

My personal branding activity has had the – very pleasant – side effect of proposals by some brands to become their ambassador. It is a nice and rewarding activity, especially because the brands with which I choose to collaborate are always consistent with my taste, my style, my image. One of the most effective ways to build your brand is to stand alongside brands that are well known by the public (that have what in technical jargon is called a greater 'brand awareness'). If, however, the positioning of the two brands put together is wrong, the deal is doomed to failure. That is why I only work with brands that I sincerely appreciate and that are consistent with my style, maybe luxury brands that have a hint of classic masculine elegance about them, which is perfectly in tune with mine.

In general, I never considered using my social media to talk about what people want, but rather what I wanted people to see in me. If you talk about what people want (which is mostly content related to other people's private lives or gossip in general), it certainly works in the immediate term, but it is unsustainable in the long run, unless you want to turn your private life into a reality show and that is something that certainly does not constitute personal branding. Once again it is essential not to lose sight of the authenticity and quality of the content, which is much more important than dizzying numbers. I say this because I realize that many of us are becoming slaves to 'likes' and to our number of followers. Using social media only as a tool to increase your visibility has nothing to do with personal branding: gossip does not create engagement, and from a marketing point of view it is absolutely useless. In fact, I would say that it is even harmful: by engaging in it you stop being a leader or influencer because you become influenced by what others tell you to appreciate. In this way, you become a follower in the proper sense of the word, because you slavishly follow the path indicated by the masses through their likes.

Gossip does not create engagement, and from a marketing point of view it is absolutely useless. Quality, coherence and authenticity are the only currencies that always pay.

Since I know that being an influencer is one of the new jobs available and that so-called 'influencer marketing' is such an incredibly serious thing, regardless of what those may think who have not yet understood how important new media has become for companies, I want to conclude by mentioning that today, companies, especially large and well-established ones, do not look at numbers but at the quality of content and positioning. They want real stories and an authentic and original point of view. I am a demonstration of this: I do not have huge numbers in the competitive arena of the world of influencers, but I am offered many high-level collaborations because of my personal branding to which I have devoted myself for years and which has made me known for what I am, both as a professional and as a person.

My professional career and also my experience with social networks have taught me that quality, coherence and authenticity are the only currencies that always pay.

CHIARA MAGNAGHI Project Manager, Condé Nast Social Talent Agency

What personal branding means

I remember very well the first time I heard of 'personal branding'. It was in 2013 when I was doing a master's degree in marketing, communication and digital strategy. The lessons were part of a module aimed at helping students to position themselves correctly and effectively within the labour market. For me who, as a law graduate and after an initial experience with *The Blonde Salad*, had decided to start from scratch following my passion for communication, it was a subject of crucial importance. It is well known that the qualifications of someone who is young and lacking in work experience are amongst the first pieces of information that a company will look at. It is therefore easy to imagine how carefully I followed those lessons, hoping to draw some useful elements to better direct my professional path.

It was then that I understood the concept behind personal branding: it is marketing but applied to the person. That is when you begin to treat yourself like a brand, starting with strategy and asking yourself one question: 'How do I want the world (in my specific case, my future employer) to perceive me?'. And this question concerns not only the present but also the future. Asking yourself this means outlining a mental career path, setting yourself medium- and long-term objectives.

Was it a theoretical application of the marketing mix, the famous 4Ps? Absolutely yes! I understood then the enormous importance of looking after your LinkedIn profile, of a correct and effective writing of the curriculum, not only as regards the substance but also the formal elements, such as the font used, the alternation between bold and italic, the image that accompanies it. In essence, it is a question of transforming yourself into a product within a market where it is essential to find the correct positioning.

After a while, however, I began to understand that treating yourself as a brand in the world of work is very important, not only when you are looking for new stimuli and want to change jobs but also more generally in order to deal with any given moment of your professional life.

Speaking of personal branding, I find the definition given by Amazon's founder, president and CEO, Jeff Bezos, that it is nothing more than 'what people say about you once you're out of the room' to be really effective and enlightening. It is a thought that has helped me during many important meetings and interviews. Over the years I have discovered that it is a fundamental concept not only for recent graduates and for those who are entering the world of work for the first time but also, and perhaps even more so, for those who hold top positions in a company's organization.

Coincidentally, sometime later, during my first internship in an advertising agency, I was given a task that was considered as being 'out of scope', ie outside my specific area of expertise. It was about developing ideas and a social media editorial plan for the company's CEO. At first the task seemed thankless to me, but then I understood the importance of the subject: enhancing the image of the person representing the company means increasing its credibility, helping it to sell its products and services. Just think of the examples of large companies whose brand is associated in the mind of the consumer directly with the founder as a person: Steve Jobs and Apple or Giorgio Armani and Armani Spa, to name just a couple. The brand and the person are interlinked by a deep bond, imprinted in the mind of the consumer. Perception is fundamental and must be treated with great care, especially in the age we are living in, in which the role of social media has become fundamental.

Enhancing the image of the person representing the company means increasing its credibility, helping it to sell its products and services.

If personal branding is important for corporate giants, it is easy to imagine how important it is in the world of startups and new digital professions. When it comes to new realities, the image of the founder must be promoted even more accurately. It is not, as in the case of the giants, the maintenance of a good image, but the creation of the corporate perception. The startupper is the mind, the idea and the product he or she wants to sell, and the company is his or her creation. And it is not only a question of credibility but also of means: it is well known that, when a business is in its initial phase, it is likely resources are limited. Using yourself as an effective communication tool for the product your company wants to sell is a matter of astuteness and optimization.

The birth of new digital professions and the end of the idea of a permanent post have made personal branding a very important aspect. If you are alone in selling your profession and services, the image you communicate through your website and social channels is an element of extraordinary importance. If you are, say, a digital professional who sells social media management services for companies, your Instagram profile, including your personal profile, must be a mirror of your profession and, therefore, of the care you will offer to your customer.

I learned from Riccardo the importance of having a targeted strategy if you are a talent manager. When managing a talent/influencer, the choice of each collaboration becomes decisive. The important thing is to always bear in mind your goal, or where you want to go, while choosing the right partners and strategies to get there. For example, collaborating free of charge with certain brands that help the talent achieve positioning targets is a physiological step on the path towards the goal. It should be considered as a real investment: it means investing time and maybe even losing job opportunities, but thanks to the association with that brand your image will achieve the desired perception.

Today, being an influencer is the ultimate evolution of the concept of personal branding. It is a 'profession' that is based on the correct management of image and person. The ability to influence users through their lives, habits and style is the evolved form of this concept.

I always advise the talents at Condé Nast Social Talent Agency to embrace the new trends in the world of influencer marketing, refine their storytelling and content creation skills, and give credibility and authenticity the right degree of importance. I remind them never to lose sight of the concept of responsibility that they have towards both their followers and the brands for which they work: it is particularly important to keep this in mind, precisely because social media is a very powerful tool. I urge them to observe and monitor their own followers and to draw inspiration from them. I stress the importance of long-term cooperation, as short-term cooperation is often confusing and does not offer any real advantage. In this regard, I remind them how much the schizophrenic shift from one brand to another within the same product category can be penalizing, and how worthwhile it is to bind yourself exclusively to a single brand instead. In theory, this should be valorized financially, but it may make more sense to renounce this aspect if for some reason the conditions are not there to achieve it, because in the long run, choosing a brand and remaining faithful to it can give much greater advantages than immediate economic gratification.

In general, understanding and following the strategic direction of communication that you have chosen helps you to get noticed by the brands and therefore to have more job opportunities, because by doing so you represent a very clear target audience. Choosing a precise editorial line entails sacrifices, but in the long run it yields greater rewards. This is demonstrated by the ever greater importance that micro-influencers, who address specific market niches and have a very deep connection with their audience, have begun to have for companies.

And my final advice concerns the importance of offline: knowing how to choose the events you attend can really make a difference.

CHAPTER NINE

A fire that does not go out

- *Build something that lasts over time.*
- *Working on long-term strategies.*

Long live evolution

A company cannot remain a startup forever: either it closes down if it cannot survive the first three years of business, or it continues its journey by structuring itself definitively. This does not mean that the founder must necessarily follow the destiny of his or her creation. They can decide to stay on board and guide it in the next stages, or they can detach themselves and launch into other projects. With *The Blonde Salad* I followed the first path, since I remained at the helm as CEO for five years, seeing it go from a very small reality born from a fashion blog to a proper media company, with more than 25 people working with us. And at that time I realized that when you start having so many people under you, your job becomes managing them and trying to solve their problems. There is the whole aspect of personnel management, hiring and firing, but also patching things up when something goes wrong with a client, who obviously does not want to talk to whoever upset him or her, but with someone who is higher up and who is able to reassure them that next time things will be better. In short, it is a completely different job from what is required in the early stages of launching a business. And some people do it very well, and they are very happy to do it. Not me, though. I prefer to get my hands dirty and work on the creative aspects, rather than sitting in an armchair directing other people's work. I say this with the utmost respect for those who are capable of doing that. In life, as always, it is a matter of being able to look within yourself and recognize what you are good at and what you are not good at.

Look within yourself and recognize what you are good at and what you are not.

Manoeuvring in port and sailing in open seas

A comparison that I think is very appropriate in this regard is that between a dock pilot and a captain. Perhaps not everyone knows that, when a large ship has to leave a commercial port, it is not the captain who directs the manoeuvres, but a local expert called a dock pilot. This person, who knows all the physical elements that characterize the port extremely well – such as currents and seabed – as well as the dominant atmospheric elements like winds and tides, manoeuvres different ships and coordinates with other shunting services, such as tugs and moorers, thus performing a task that no one else would be able to carry out, thereby preventing the ship from doing or suffering damage near the coast while manoeuvring it in restricted waters.

As long as they are engaged in the manoeuvring phase, the pilot's seat is the ship's bridge. Once the ship has got under way and reached the open sea, the pilot uses the Jacob's ladder, which is a ladder of rope, to get into a smaller boat, called a pilot boat, which then brings them back to port. At that point the command of the ship passes to the captain, who commands it during navigation of the open seas to its final destination. I find this similarity fascinating, and it perfectly illustrates the differences between the launch phase of a business and the rest of its life. Both can be difficult, because there are many dangers in open sea navigation, just as there are countless pitfalls when manoeuvring in restricted waters, but what I would like to point out is that their management requires different and complementary skills. When directing *The Blonde Salad* I realized that I gave the best of myself in the first of the two phases. I was like a dock pilot... or a builder, the one who lays the foundations, builds the pillars, puts up the walls and then, when everything is complete, when even the decorations are in place, is happy to leave the keys of the building to someone else so that they can live there and administer it. And that way I can go and lay the foundations of another building!

Strategy and tactics

Of course, those who look after the initial stages of a project cannot keep their eyes fixed only on the present, but must also project into the future, even if at that point – if they are a true serial startupper – they may already be on the Jacob's ladder, about to jump off the ship. In other words, they will have to draw up a long-term action plan in order to set up and then coordinate the actions aimed at achieving the goal they had set themselves and then work concretely on the actions to be taken day after day to achieve that goal. It is the famous distinction between strategy and tactics, so dear to marketing experts and theorized more than 25 centuries ago by the legendary general Sun Tzu in his treatise *The Art of War*: 'Strategy without tactics is the slowest route to victory. Tactics without strategy are the noise before defeat'. Those who drive a startup must have a vision, then a strategy to achieve that vision and finally a tactic. The strategy identifies the long-term objectives and defines the path to achieve them; tactics are something more concrete and are oriented to the short term. Without a bigger plan, without an overall view, without a fundamental reason, in short, without a strategy, every tactic can in actual fact do more harm than good. Disregarding a long-term vision risks crystallizing organizational action into short-sighted short-term management in which management choices are made on the basis of changing circumstances, thus exposing the company to a high risk of inconsistency.

Without a bigger plan, without an overall view, tactics may do · more harm than good.

The strategic plan, drawn up in order to make its vision a reality, must remain fixed for at least six months, while the tactical plan is drawn up day by day. To return to the nautical comparison, I would say that the vision can be equated to the decision to reach the Caribbean from Genoa. The strategy is to go through the Strait of Gibraltar, and then point north and so on. The tactic is to cast off the moorings, follow the course closely, haul aft the mainsail... in short, all those practical operations necessary to bring the boat closer to its destination.

Returning to the business environment, a good example in this sense can be the one provided by Apple. I believe that Apple's vision was to bring design into the field of technology and monopolize the digital life of (potential) customers with their products. The strategy was to design a series of devices that would 'cover' all possible uses: when you relax on the sofa with your iPad, when you are on the subway with your iPhone, when you arrive at the office with your Mac, when you go for a jog with your Apple Watch. The tactic has been to concretely realize the various versions of all these products. I have the impression that, since Steve Jobs died, only the tactics have remained... and that the vision and strategy have been a bit lost along the way. Proof of this is the fact that, since he has gone, no new products have been launched, only new versions of existing products. It has to be said that it is also physiological that a company's driving force runs out, but something suggests to me that Jobs' creative drive would not have done so and that, had he survived, he would probably have known how to invent something new.

Learning to say goodbye

Obviously, even if you know your talent lies in being a dock pilot, making that leap and abandoning the bridge of command can be difficult. Accepting the fact that a creation of yours starts to walk in a different direction from the one you had laid out for it is not very easy to manage from a psychological point of view, because that reality was born out of your vision. And to create it, investments were made and a series of tactical actions were put in place that you, as founder, worked hard on. Investors are aware of this reality, incidentally. It is not uncommon for them to make it a condition of their investment that the founder or founders undertake to respect a lock-in clause, that is not to leave the project for a predetermined period, which usually lasts five years. This is because, as I hope I have made clear, generally the investment is made not so much just in the company but also in the vision of the founder in particular, so it is natural that investors want him or her to remain involved in the project for as long as possible.

Accepting the fact that a creation of yours starts to walk in a different direction from the one you had laid out for it is difficult.

And I have to admit that, even when all our obligations to investors have been met, it is not easy to leave your creation in the hands of someone else, as anyone knows who has been in the situation of closing one chapter of their life to start another. This is because inevitably you feel attached to what you have created, even if you may also feel a strong desire to take on new challenges. They are two contrasting and equally powerful pulls, not least because as long as you stay with your project you have a goal, a mission... and, let's admit it, you are also within the confines of a comfort zone, while abandoning it means putting yourself back into play, seeing if you are capable of doing something else and even facing the risk of not being able to do so. After leaving *The Blonde Salad* I deliberately spent a few months doing nothing, because I was convinced that it would be the best way to regain energy and stimulation. After so many years living at a hundred miles an hour, it was not easy to get used to such carefree idleness, but it was really therapeutic.

In those months I learned that if you have motivation inside you, that fire will never go out and you can always begin again with another project, more energetically than before. If you do not have motivation inside you, I do not know whether you can find it by yourself. I definitely know that it helps a lot to have role models. For me, the first was undoubtedly my mother, who among all my mentors was the most important and who showed me, even before telling me, what it means to work hard, to not be defeated by any difficulty and to have an unshakable work ethic. One thing I would like to say, however, is that those who do not feel that they have this drive inside should not think that they are less than those who do have it. I am not exalting the startupper, nor the hyperactive, a category to which I admit I belong, to the detriment of all others. The important thing is to look in the mirror with serenity and understand where your energies can best be spent. Not everyone will have that motivation, but everyone definitely has characteristics that will allow them to find satisfaction in life if they put in the right effort. If carried out with poetry, masterpieces can emerge from any activity.

After all, the life of the startupper is, as I have said several times, beautiful in many ways but very hard in others and requires many sacrifices. Of course, you also need to learn to use your time efficiently and not think that you need to always work more than 12 hours a day, as I hear many people say with a mixture of pride and victimhood. The results of the work are not necessarily measured by the hours we devote to it. Today, after so many years of hard work, I notice that sometimes I get more done in two hours than in a day of 12 hours. If I manage to create connections between people, pull out ideas.... I know that I certainly would not have got to that point if I had not had so many years of 12-hour days behind me, but the important thing is to be aware that not all your working life has to be like that!

Self-confidence is not arrogance

Accepting yourself for what you are, recognizing your limits and your potential, means moving towards professional choices that are undoubtedly more satisfying and more in line with the person you really are. Strengthened by this awareness, you can present yourself to the world of work with confidence in yourself and your own means, without being arrogant. In my professional career I have been helped, among other things, by an absolute lack of timidity. This is a gift of character, but I believe that an even more decisive role has been played by certain rules of good manners, for which once again I must thank my mother, which have allowed me to always feel at ease in all situations. I have found myself in front of objectively extraordinary people, who in their field have achieved incredible success and created something monumental. Those rules of conduct that I had learned allowed me to feel relaxed, to never feel embarrassed. If you know how to behave, you can always adapt to the environment in which you find yourself and you will never be out of place, because you have certainties you can rely on. I never feel fear in front of those who are superior to me, but only enthusiasm at the idea of being able to meet someone who has so much to teach me. It seems that some people have qualms in admitting that they are in an inferior position, which does not mean putting themselves down or ignoring their own value, but rather recognizing that you are faced with a person who has undertaken a professional or human journey worthy of admiration, and from whom you can only learn. Other than that, you have to play your role, whatever it is, with your head held high and learn to look everyone in the eye, giving them all the respect they deserve. It is not only a question of common sense and humanity but also, banally, of practice. In a world where roles, unlike in the past, are so fragile and the landscape of work so fluid and changing, those who know how to do things have already won.

LUCIANO BERNARDINI DE PACE   Editor of *Rolling Stone* Italy

Can a 62-year-old man who has had everything in life – love, money and personal success – reinvent himself and start over again?

The answer is yes, if he can see the train passing and jump on it. It happened to me the day after I liquidated, selling 40 years of work for the sum of six million euros, cash, and at a stroke! At that precise moment – it was April 2014 – and with that amount in my pocket, I could have stopped and retired, but instead I saw the train passing emblazoned with the most powerful and irreverent brand in the history of counterculture and of the revolutionary generation of the US 1970s, *Rolling Stone*, which was to cease publishing in our country that very month.

That day I jumped on the train that was taking that magazine to the cemetery of Italian publishing and communication and I made it change direction. Vision? Madness? Entrepreneurship? Bravery? Presumption? Character? All of it when, on 1 May of the same year, in New York, I acquired the licence for the publishing and communication sector of *Rolling Stone*.

Can a 62-year-old man who has had everything in life reinvent himself and start over again? The answer is yes, if he can see the train passing and jump on it.

In Italy *Rolling Stone* was an old brand, even obsolete, sold on the advertising market for a few euros per page... but it had the strength of a unique brand. The mentality and business model of the other publishers, at a time of apparent crisis in the sector, were based on the defence of the past, while I, following not the crisis but the evolution of the communication sector, could attack the future.

I had nothing to lose but the six million euros I had in my pocket. Money is a material thing, success is an aphrodisiac... and getting such a buzz at 65 years old is pure ecstasy. Seeing is believing. From old nostalgic rock to pop culture, from just music to real life, from the fetishist fanaticism of the past to the discovery of the future. I studied the technology that changes our lives, I took note of the dramatic reduction of the generation gap, I invested in the megaphones of social media and the web. I turned a brand from the past into a perspective for the future, I invested in content. I listened to a lot of people, but I acted according to my own logic. I looked for inexperienced young people and some of them were spoiled by well-being... but those hungry for success and competition have made the difference. The aim has always and only been to represent true reality, combined with behavioural ethics and intellectual honesty: respect first for the reader (my new boss) and then for the

I have not forgotten the past, which remains an intense experience, and I have ridden the present to build the future.

client. The money comes from the client, but if you win over a reader, he will not let you go and you will make clean money. I have not forgotten the past, which remains an intense experience, and I have ridden the present to build the future. I think it works in many fields, not just in publishing. Maybe I spent a few sleepless nights, but in the morning the desire and determination to achieve the result produced tons of adrenaline. I never gave up, and in the meantime, I had Pannella, a prime minister, the Pope and Bebe Vio, who is an example of life for everyone, on my front covers. Not just rock music... but pop culture.

CHAPTER TEN

So have you made it now?

- *Success and failure.*
- *Human and social factors by which success is measured.*
- *How startups are changing the world.*
- *Experience at Harvard Business School.*

In bankruptcy school

If even Master Yoda, in the eighth instalment of the *Star Wars* saga, *The Last Jedi*, says that: 'Failure is the greatest teacher', you have to believe it. I know it can just be a turn of phrase, a mere consolation for those who have not seen an idea they believed in take off, but I firmly believe that failure is a great resource and that you can only get to success through failure. Additionally, the fact that a project goes wrong does not mean that the person has failed, just that the project in question has failed. If anything, you have to be good at understanding when to give up, to avoid throwing money away and continuing slavishly at something that does not work. It takes the right sensitivity to understand when to close a chapter and open a new one. Three or four of my companies went out of business in the first three years after they were set up, but then three went well. My three successful companies have largely recouped the losses of those that went wrong, so in the end the balance is positive from the point of view of the value created. And it is normal that it should

The fact that a project goes wrong does not mean that the person has failed but that the project has failed.

go like that. I started when I was 20, when I did not even know what startup meant and I did things just because I wanted to do them. From those failures, however, I drew some important lessons that have remained engraved in my mind and that guide me in my entrepreneurial choices.

In 2013, for example, Stefano and I founded a brand of pocket handkerchiefs for men's jackets, called Ferrucci Milano. The idea came from the fact that both he and I liked to put them in the pockets of elegant and sporty jackets, and we realized that there was no dedicated brand. There were those without brands – very simple affairs without any personality – and those produced by the historic brands of ties and silk scarves. We therefore decided to create a specific line of casual chic pocket handkerchiefs, very recognizable, bright colours and fresh and original patterns, with very special packaging, giving a touch of originality to the male style.

The project was well thought out and the brand was good, so we started to do some public relations work to introduce the product and found, in fact, that customers also liked it. At that time, however, we were both very busy with other activities, me with *The Blonde Salad* and Stefano with his work in a multinational company. We simply hired an intern to take care of the more operational part, but there was no one to put in the energy, passion and love necessary to get the company off the ground, because we founders were dedicating ourselves to something else. So Ferrucci Milano continued for one or two years, dragging its heels. We threw a lot of money at it because we were nevertheless trying to achieve something, but we lost too many opportunities, and in the end, we decided to suspend the project.

From this experience of failure I learned that when launching a project, you have to be 100 per cent focused. Now I know that when you set up a new company, in addition to the idea and the money, you also need a person who is ready to devote all their time and energy to it. Even in the launch phase of Foorban I was very busy as CEO of TBS Crew and the Chiara Ferragni Collection. And I am convinced that even that project would have gone wrong if there had not been someone willing to devote all their energy to it, even though the idea was right, there was no shortage of money and everything was ready to go. In that case, however, I knew that I could count on my partners, who were willing to give all of themselves to that new activity, embodying its soul.

Another story of 'failure' from which I learned a lot was that of Werelse, an online platform that I launched, again with Stefano, in 2011. It was used to present products that Chiara Ferragni and two other international bloggers – Andy Torres of StyleScrapbook and Carolina Engman of Fashion Squad, who at the time were similar to her in terms of numbers – designed in collaboration with various brands. In practice it was a platform where it was possible to buy limited-edition capsule collections designed by three of the most famous and followed fashion bloggers of the time. The idea looked a bit like what is now the shop section of

Even interesting or indeed potentially revolutionary projects risk failure if they are launched when the market is not ready for them.

The Blonde Salad, that is an e-commerce where you can buy customized capsule collections. At the time, however, it was a project that was a little too innovative for the market to get a handle on and therefore we struggled to persuade companies to participate. When we did manage to, the collections went well, like the Mango Touch accessories collection, but overall the business was too complex, and the results did not equate to the efforts, so we decided to shut it down.

The Werelse experience taught me that timing is everything, that even interesting or indeed potentially revolutionary projects risk failure if they are launched when the market is not ready for them. And that patience is a virtue you must never forget!

What is success? What is failure?

I think we should agree once and for all what the two terms 'success' and 'failure' really mean. Because I think that the idea that prevails in contemporary society is absolutely misleading and is making us completely forget where personal success really lies, bombarding us with the false concept that money is the only real yardstick.

Maybe it is a bit strange that I am the one who says this, who until now has worked mainly in the world of fashion and luxury and who is certainly not a do-gooder. However, even what I did in that sector was marked by a certain vision of the business. Maybe I could have earned a lot more, or maybe I would not have got to where I did… it is impossible to know. What is certain is that I did not co-found *The Blonde Salad* and Foorban to get rich, but to do something I liked and was passionate about, following my ethics. In the end, that is all that matters to me.

Of course, thanks to the positive results I have obtained, I have reached economic security earlier than the average of my peers with some of my activities, and I have been able to cater to a lot of whims at an age when it is usually difficult to do so, unless you can count on family money. But I am sincerely convinced that my greatest riches, beyond the house, a nice car or the possibility to travel – which I appreciate very much! – are my experience and the network I have created. These are things that I have built up slowly and cultivated over the last seven years… and I believe and hope that they will be the ones to serve me in the future.

Tear down the walls… even those covered in chiffon

Another great satisfaction is to be able to say that we have helped to change in some way the rules of a closed, elitist and apparently untouchable sector like fashion. In fact, there is no doubt that the impact of fashion blogs such as *The Blonde Salad* on the world of fashion and in particular luxury has been very strong.

That was something I noticed within the first few months of *The Blonde Salad*'s life. Even before the blog existed, her photos, posted on social networks, attracted the attention of thousands of users. The incredible thing was that even on a photo-sharing site like Flickr, where many professional photographers posted and shared their shots, Chiara's photos often managed to attract more interest than theirs. It was rather surprising to see how selfies made with few technical means by a girl from the Italian provinces were more liked than photoshoots carried out in exotic locations by international professionals at considerable expense in time, energy and resources.

The reason why it happened is unfathomable and I can only attribute it to the so-called 'x-factor', that certain *je ne sais quoi* that is impossible to describe that some people have and that manages to attract the attention of others. Certainly, some aspects have helped a lot: the fact that her features correlated to a canon of beauty appreciated worldwide; the fact that she was good looking but not as unapproachable as a supermodel, with that girl-next-door charm; and the fact that she was Italian, so in a sense an expert in fashion 'by birthright', but nevertheless with an international profile. As did the fact that she came from a normal background and had a life and experiences that were easy to identify with, elements that in the boom years of reality shows were fundamental. The interest generated by Chiara and other fashion bloggers then joined forces with the so-called peer-to-peer effect, which was that if they were wearing a garment or an accessory, it was not perceived as advertising but as the advice of a friend who had suggested buying a product.

I dedicated my degree thesis to this topic, which I discussed in 2010 at the Bocconi University. During my research I had proposed two images to a wide target of people belonging to the same statistical cluster: the first was a Chanel bag worn by Chiara; the second was the same bag worn by a model in an editorial for an iconic fashion magazine. I then asked the members of the research group several questions to understand whether willingness to spend, desire to make the purchase, confidence in the brand, perception of the usefulness of the product, varied or not depending on the image they were seeing. And, needless to say, those who saw the picture of the bag worn by Chiara felt a closeness to the brand that in the other case was not as strong. And they also perceived a completely different usefulness of the product. This also happened with younger girls of limited finan-cial means, who expressed a desire to save up to buy that designer bag, knowing they could also use it in combination with extremely casual clothing, perhaps purchased in low-cost chains.

In fact, one of the great innovations brought about by the fash-ion bloggers was to render acceptable the idea that you do not need to dress from head to toe in designer clothes, that you can easily combine a designer bag with torn jeans or a pair of canvas trainers. This acknowledgement of the mix and match phenome-non has become fashionable thanks to fashion bloggers and influencers, and has greatly favoured luxury brands, because it has brought them closer to a new consumer group. Even young people, who cannot afford to have a wardrobe full of designer clothes, save to buy even one piece that they perceive as iconic and that they no longer feel as being so far removed from them and their world. That is why luxury brands have ridden this phenomenon, which has been a great privilege to live and help create.

You must always try to stay one step ahead of time in order to seize the most advantageous opportunities.

What we have achieved in the world of fashion, anticipating a trend that has since become widely diffused and inserting ourselves in a space that at that time barely existed, is what every entrepreneur should wish to be able to do: balancing instinct and experience, trying to always stay one step ahead of time in order to seize the most advantageous opportunities.

Faster than light

Speaking of low-cost chain stores, awareness is growing of the human, social and environmental costs of many companies that create fast fashion, that is, those that produce and sell cheap and fashionable items, constantly proposing new ones. Their production rates are sustainable only by moving factories to countries where labour costs are low, where in many cases the safety conditions of workers are not optimal, and respect for norms governing the acquisition of raw materials, production, transport and disposal of the product to reduce environmental impact are rather erratic. Today there are consumers who show a certain sensibility towards and consciousness of these issues and who therefore pay more attention to the origin of the materials and where the clothes are made. However, this discourse concerns a cultural elite, which is not very relevant in percentage terms. Also, the speed and pervasiveness of the means of communication available to us today have made the changing of trends and the continuous diffusion of new fashions even faster, which in terms of clothing translates into a notable superficiality. In other words, today's mass market clothing is all image and little substance – as long as a garment is cute, fashionable and looks good when worn, it does not matter whether it is of good quality or durable. After all, today's youngsters were born with Snapchat and Instagram, so it is understandable that for them the period of use for a garment would be equivalent to the handful of seconds that a video posted online lasts.

It is undeniable that in the spread of fast fashion there is at least one positive aspect, which is that of having democratized style, making it more accessible and allowing people, especially the young, to have large and varied wardrobes. The costs of luxury brands are in fact untenable for the majority of consumers. While they make sense in terms of the originality of the designs, the quality of the materials and the rigour of the production methods, it is also true that they are dictated by marketing, respond to a precise pricing strategy and are not justifiable in terms of production costs alone.

I think that, in the future, the elite that is more sensitized to these issues will influence the vision and therefore the choices of the masses, which will gradually evolve. At least, that is the way it has always been. I am an optimist and for me it is natural to think that society is evolving and not regressing. In this vein I see the increasingly growing trend towards transparency in the world of fashion, so there are many new companies that are placed somewhere in the middle between the two extremes of high fashion and fast fashion, making lovely, good quality products at fair prices.

One such case is of a very interesting Italian startup founded by Simone Maggi and Riccardo Schiavotto, called Lanieri. Once again it is an example of how tradition and innovation can coexist, under the banner of Made in Italy and craftsmanship. Their project was born of the desire to respond to a male need: that of being able to have clothes and shirts made to measure, tailored, of great quality and at prices that are more affordable than is normally the case for such products. Lanieri combines the excellence of Italian tailoring with a very innovative multichannel way of selling, which allows you to buy both online and in the Atelier. It is a really good project that is enjoying great success throughout Europe and that will soon be extended to the United States. This, plus its young and motivated team, has led to traditional businesses and leaders in fabrics, such as Reda among others, to believe and invest in it. The first time you go to the Atelier to have your measurements taken, a virtual card is created and then, from there, you can order both in store and through the website, customizing the desired item in every detail and seeing straight away what the finished product will look like, which will then be delivered to your home or to the store. They are beautiful clothes, which I often wear and receive many compliments for every time, that have competitive prices despite the high quality, and allow anyone, regardless of where they are physically, to buy a tailored product.

A promised land, a different world

Lanieri is just one of many examples of how the digital revolution has changed and still is changing consumption, a reality that we all experience every day.

One of the characteristics of the economic model called the sharing economy, which is spreading more and more – and in increasingly wide and diversified sectors – is that it has shifted the focus from the sale of a product to the offer of a service (from the point of view of those who provide it) and from the possession of one's own item to the use of a common

One of the characteristics of the sharing economy is that it has shifted the focus from ownership to service.

good (by those who use it). It is an epoch-making change, which is revolutionizing our lifestyles and introducing new ones, favouring savings, socialization and, in some cases, the safeguarding of the environment.

I am thinking, for example, of a car-sharing method such as Car2go, which has completely changed the concept of mobility, even more than other services have done, such as the one offered by Uber, which has also been revolutionary in many ways due to its size. In Italy, the options UberBlack, UberLux and UberVan are currently active, which allow the rental through the app of a sedan or a van with a professional driver, while in many other countries of the world UberX is also active, where you can get lifts from private individuals. It can be said, therefore, that Uber has 'simply' put customers in touch with drivers and that, in countries where UberX is active, has regulated and made easier a custom as old as the car itself, that of offering and asking for lifts... making life for those who have to move around the city and who do not have a car, or even a licence, much easier, and allowing private individuals to earn some money (where it is allowed) and professional drivers to fill the lulls that traditionally occur between one customer and another.

Car2go has introduced a brand new element in the transport sector, because it has rendered obsolete the idea that it is necessary to own a means of transport to move about – using the app you can find the nearest available car on the map of the city, and the rental period begins when you get in the car and ends when you arrive at your destination. The fact that it is an innovative and sensational concept is demonstrated by the wave of startups offering a similar or parallel car-sharing service, such as DriveNow or Enjoy, but also by the fact that many companies, starting with the same idea, are trying to improve it.

This is the case with Fair, which for the moment exists only in the United States where it is enjoying great success. You pay a monthly subscription to always have a car available, you can stop it at any time and, if you want a better equipped or more powerful car, you can upgrade through the app. The service takes care of collecting the car you no longer want and possibly replacing it with another... and all this at much lower costs than those usually faced by the owner of a car or those who decide to rent a car for a short period. Fair works a bit like Netflix, whose subscription costs vary depending on the number of devices you want to use. In this case the figure varies depending on the type of car you want, with the ability to upgrade and downgrade according to your needs.

All this could not have happened without the experience of Car2go, which not only created a better way to move about but gave everyone the chance to be the owner of the transport, without the need to own the car. It meant digitizing the ownership of the car, or rather making it actually pointless, and thus initiating a radical paradigm shift in the economy because it rendered access to a service more important than the ownership of an object.

I am convinced that we will get to a point where manufacturers will only sell cars to these companies and no longer to private individuals. Obviously, this does not mean that no one will own cars anymore, because there will always be enthusiasts as well as collectors. And in fact I imagine that people will tend to own vintage cars, which are more aesthetically beautiful and more fun for enthusiasts because they are not as perfect from a technical point of view as the new ones (and I will be one of them!).

This innovative approach, which is just one of the many manifestations of the sharing economy, is continuously extending even to goods other than cars. For example, there are already those who offer – to a mainly female clientele – the rental of particularly expensive garments and accessories for a limited time. An example of this is the US company Rent the Runway, which offers various subscription formulas and is enjoying huge success. For example, with a US $89 dollar monthly subscription, you can choose four items that are available to you for 30 days. After choosing the garment on the internet, you order it and it is delivered to your home fresh from the laundry. The ordered items are used and, once the rental period has elapsed, they are sent back at no additional cost. Apart from convenience, it is a way to invite consumers to behave more responsibly, limiting the number of garments that are purchased and then end up languishing in the closet after just a few uses.

A similar service began a couple of years ago in Italy, with the startup Front Row Tribe, which was launched by Olimpia Pitacco and Gabriela Pacini and offers the possibility to rent elegant and designer clothes through a website (although there is also a store in Milan), with delivery, laundry and, if necessary, tailoring services. The rental lasts four days and is perfect for those who have to attend an important event and need the right outfit. Until a few years ago, it would have seemed unthinkable, perhaps even unseemly, to do such a thing! Instead, now that consumer culture has got us used to buying what we need for a special occasion only to never wear it again, it makes ever more sense to spend money on renting a beautiful high-fashion dress rather than spending the same amount on buying a less beautiful, less well-kept and less original dress, maybe from a low-cost chain.

In the field of men's clothing the approach is different: the man can buy a beautiful outfit made well and even invest a few euros more because he will use it on many occasions. For women, on the other hand, clothes are often a matter of status symbols. They are used to amaze on a special occasion and that is all. So there is no need to own them! Again, such a concept is not applicable to collectors, but that is a niche: I am convinced that for the mass market the cultural paradigm is changing, and how.

And the fact that the world is changing thanks to new technologies is not perceived only in the light of market changes, because new technologies have endless applications, even in the social media sector. When I am in New York, I sometimes use a very nice app called DEED, whose slogan is 'Do something good today' and whose purpose is to make volunteering easy, fun and social.

It allows the user to find out about the activities taking place in a certain place and at a certain time, so that they can take part to help someone. They range from taking dogs out of a kennel to distributing meals to the homeless: those who want to, can help.

Taking the podium

Entering into the job market at a time of such profound transformation has allowed me to set up some successful businesses. I believe that those who find themselves living in periods of revolution have an advantage over those who work in a static context, because these are the moments in which you can really innovate and do something great. The fact that some of the activities I have been involved in over the years have gone so well is obviously a great satisfaction, but I would not be an entrepreneur, and certainly not a serial one, if I ever thought I had arrived, had made it. My hope is that in my life I will continue to chase after good and interesting projects that will always teach me something new.

Those who live in periods of revolution have an advantage over those who work in a static context.

Usually when someone says: 'I've made it', they stop doing, so I hope with all my heart that for me that day will never come. If you do things with only an economic objective in mind, this drive will dry up very quickly. As I said, you should not do business to get rich, but for passion. The terms of the question must, if anything, be reversed: only if you have passion, a vision, a dream, will you find the energy to pursue something until you probably turn it into a success story... that will also generate profits. When the approach is the other way round, things are much less simple, because at a certain point, on the tenth night in a row spent working, maybe editing photos for a blog as in my case, without seeing even a penny – because it is normal that in that phase money has not started to come in yet – fatigue and discouragement enter the fray and maybe start you thinking about starting the next project.

Usually when someone says 'I've made it', they stop doing, so I hope with all my heart that for me that day will never come.

Of course there have been some small and some big moments of exaltation along the way, also because the sector in which I have mainly worked over these years, that of fashion, has allowed me to travel a lot, to live out of the ordinary experiences, to touch stardust with my own hands, which, let us admit it, makes life a little more enjoyable. For example, I remember when my supervisor for my thesis, Emanuela Prandelli, called me to yell at me because I had not gone to her to review the data, and I answered her, 'Professor, Dior sent a limo to pick me up, how could I say no? I'll be there next week!'.

But those moments were never the substance of what I was doing, nor the reason why I was doing it. Apart from these folkloric and enjoyable episodes, I remember above all the hard work of that period.

And that is why the greatest satisfaction I have had so far has been the invitation received in 2014 from the professors of the MBA (Master's in Business Administration) at Harvard Business School, who had decided to give the case study of *The Blonde Salad* to their students. Through a series of telephone interviews, a meeting in London and many email exchanges, we collaborated in the drafting of the presentation, retracing our history with the Harvard teachers. Then the professors presented the case to their students who, divided into groups, worked on it, imagining different possible developments for our business. At the time, in fact, the fashion blog from which everything started had already evolved into a lifestyle magazine and we had launched our collection of shoes and accessories. The task of the students, as is generally the case in a business school, was to come up with ideas on how our business could grow further. In February 2015, the case study was finally presented in the lecture hall.

I was very excited that day: less than four years after the discussion of my degree thesis, the company I had helped to found had become a subject of study in one of the most prestigious universities in the world. A Harvard case study, like the ones I had studied at the Bocconi.

Less than four years after I had graduated, the company I had helped found had become a subject of study at one of the most prestigious universities in the world.

When we arrived in Cambridge, Massachusetts, we were greeted by a very strong icy wind, it was bitterly cold and it must have been 15 degrees below zero, which is the norm there in winter. To help us settle in, the students took us on a tour of the campus and it was a lot of fun. The next day we met the professors who had chosen our case and we had lunch with them. But I was really tense and hardly ate anything. The nervousness melted when we entered the lecture hall, where the students, who were our peers, welcomed us. After the presentation of the various projects there was a debate, which was particularly stimulating, and Chiara and I gave feedback on the various projects. In particular, one of the groups had imagined the launch of e-commerce, which was what we were also working on during that period. So we continued to work with that group, which in the end chose *The Blonde Salad* case as the subject of their final thesis project.

In February 2017 we were invited back to Harvard. Obviously, the emotion was always great, but not comparable to that of the first time, because this time I was much more relaxed.

I took the podium myself to tell the students what had happened with *The Blonde Salad* in the meantime and what our future growth strategies were. I dealt with issues that were delicate and more linked to marketing theory, such as the use of social media and the strategies aimed at depersonalizing the business.

The interesting thing was that, on that occasion, we had the opportunity to share an observation – in the most prestigious of contexts and at the highest possible level for those who deal with these issues – on a critical point that at the beginning of our adventure together we could never even have imagined. And it was the fact that we had had different points of view on the future development of our project (that Chiara, for obvious reasons, has always seen in very personal terms, whereas I would have preferred to consolidate our role even more within the world of fashion), which led us a few months later to interrupt our collaboration.

Knowing that the most important business school in the world has proposed your company to its students as a subject of study, because it represents an innovative model that has generated a great change in the fashion and communication sector, is an immense honour. But, as I see it, great successes give rise to great responsibility. If I have managed to achieve such a result, I must work hard to go forward and do even better. That is why for me it was not a point of arrival, but a point of departure.

PIERRE-YVES WECXSTEEN   General Manager, Chanel European Fashion

When it comes to brand image, the two most important words are: no compromises! You can play with the brand identity, but the most important challenge remains knowing how to evaluate this thin line beyond which you lose your soul.

Conclusion

From zero to infinity

How do you start from scratch after a success or failure?

In recent times, the generation of lifelong entrepreneurs has come to an end, and it is inevitable that you must be ready, over time, to undertake more than one project and have the lucidity to temper the passion necessary to set them up while not becoming too attached to a single perspective. This is true for everyone: whether your business experience has failed or has been crowned with success, at a certain point it is likely that you will need to break away from it and have the cool-headedness to understand either that it is better to close it or, on the other hand, that the business must leave the startup phase in order to grow.

I realize that the psychological state of those who, for various reasons, decide to move away from their successful project to undertake another one is very different from that of someone who has had to close their project because it has failed. With the latter, the knockback can be very hard: it is difficult to shake off the guilt, frustration or belief that you have done something wrong, even if it may not always be the case as the reasons why a business goes wrong can be innumerable.

On the other hand, it is undeniable that in every project there is a certain level of uncertainty, because chance exists and can play out both positively and negatively... and while in the first case fortune can help, though generally does not change the outcome of things, in the second case bad luck can actually undermine you. You may do everything right and fail anyway because of bad luck. I do not think the opposite is true, that you can be lucky enough to do everything badly and still be successful. Luck can give you a prod, but if things do not evolve because you do not know how to progress them, then they simply will not evolve. The influence of the chance factor can be reduced by controlling all the other variables, something generally acquired through experience because you become better at understanding the needs of the market, anticipating changes, managing staff, administering everything related to the effectiveness and timing of a certain business and, especially, at learning from your mistakes.

In any case, it is inevitable that those who have invested all their time and energy in a project and are forced to close it, will suffer. Luckily, I have never found myself in this situation, because the startups that I have launched and that went wrong had not absorbed 100 per cent of my resources, but in fact were side projects compared to the main ones (and, as I explained earlier, this was at least partly the reason why they failed).

A company is a living animal that can change and even make mistakes, stumble and rise again, but it certainly cannot stand still.

From my own experience, however, I can say that it is also painful to move away from a company that you have founded and that is going well, as happened to me at the end of 2017 when I decided to leave all the operational positions within the TBS Crew and to maintain only the role of adviser. The certainty that my partner and I no longer shared the same vision for our company made my decision easier: rather than leave what I had built in a stalemate, I preferred to take a step back. Because nothing is more harmful to a company than stagnation: a company is a living animal that can change and even make mistakes, stumble and rise again, but it certainly cannot stand still.

This conviction has not prevented me from feeling a certain melancholy, as happens every time a phase of life comes to an end, especially when it has been crammed with adventures, rich in satisfaction, full of commitments as well as studded with many sacrifices. It is a very human feeling, but I think that when you find yourself in situations like this, it is important not to fall into the trap of thinking that you were destined to do that one thing and nothing else. This is a discourse that applies not just to me but also to everyone else, and it is not relevant only to the workplace. When something ends, it is not the end of everything; it was not the only opportunity in life, it was just one of many. Those who have the passion and desire can always start again, writing a new chapter in their history and shaping the reality around them. And, if it is true that a work project, for those who conceived and built it, is a bit like having a child, then we must remember that nothing prevents us from having more than one child in the space of a lifetime!

Those who have the passion and desire can always start again, writing a new chapter in their history and shaping the reality around them.

Passion is the proverbial lever that raises the world. And probably, if you are doing what you are passionate about, you do not even need to read this book. Because you will already know how to put your vision into practice, endure the inevitable sacrifices, motivate your team and make the right decisions for your business. I am sure that no gain or security is as important as being happy with what you are doing. So, if there is something out there that you love, if you know that there is a project that can get you up in the morning with an energy you did not even know you had, chase it with all your strength and determination.

Index